PRAISE

"In our brain-based economy we too often fail to value powerful lessons from the heart! Johnny Covey's book can be your instruction manual for a heart-guided life filled with immense joy and purposeful contribution. Read this book; your heart will thank you for what it now gets to do…and, so will your head!"

~**Chip R. Bell,** bestselling author of *Sprinkles: Creating Awesome Experiences Through Innovative Service*

"*5 Habits to Lead from Your Heart* is a most helpful playbook for anyone looking to proactively make better choices in work and in life. It is yet another winner in the Covey tradition."

~**Doug Conant,** Founder & CEO, Conant Leadership and former CEO, Campbell Soup and Chairman, Avon Products

"Johnny Covey's *5 Habits to Lead from Your Heart* help us play the game of life by identifying when we are in our head and when we are coming from our heart. Johnny guides us how to do what we know we should do—by changing how we think and feel—and then mentors us how to exercise courage, choose our experience, and become a conscious creator of our own lives."

~**Marilyn McLeod,** executive coach and author of *Global Mindset Leadership*

"Well done, Johnny! *5 Habits to Lead from Your Heart* is a rare wake-up call in our search for meaning. I found myself compelled to share this book with extended family and friends."

~**Greg Link,** co-author of *Smart Trust*, Co-founder CoveyLink

"I just finished reading Johnny's *5 Habits to Lead from Your Heart*. My impression: *5 Habits* is a game changer! Having coached championship rugby teams for two decades, I know what a difference "playing from the heart" makes on the field. *5 Habits* is the perfect playbook for coaching us to see why we do what we do and how to wisely choose both our responses and our experiences to align what we know and believe with what we think, feel and do."

~**Larry Gelwix,** CEO, Columbus Travel, subject of the film and author of *Forever Strong*

"Stephen R. Covey's rich legacy of personal achievement has stood the test of time, and only becomes stronger as his son Stephen M.R. Covey and now Johnny Covey help us extend and apply it in their own unique ways. As we all strive mightily to cope with the strange world this new millennium has thrust us into, we must stay in touch with the core of our humanity. The *5 Habits to Lead from Your Heart*, as Johnny calls them, may ultimately be our only real survival strategy."

~**Karl Albrecht,** Ph.D., author of *Social Intelligence: The New Science of Success*

"Johnny's profound insights inspire courage to change as you recognize the truth about who you really are—a worthy, accepted and valuable being of divine origin. His way of sharing hits home."

~**Dr. Bradley Nelson,** bestselling author of *The Emotion Code*

"If you want a book that is bone honest, practical, personal and profound, this is it. No sugar coating—just real help for real problems."

~**Scott C. Hammond,** author of *Lessons of the Lost:*
Finding Hope and Resilience in Work/Life

"Books on self-development are too numerous to count but occasionally one stands out in its utter simplicity and practicality. If you seek positive change in any or all aspects of your life, you need only read and apply what is outlined in this one book. Yes, it is that important!"

~**Susanne Biro,** leadership coach
and co-author of *Unleashed! The Leader as Coach*

"This is an extraordinary book that helps you travel the journey from doing to being, from planning to achieving, and from success to significance. It teaches. It coaches. It inspires. You'll love the substantive content and the substantial treatment on how you can be all you are intended to be. Enjoy."

~**Dr. Nido Qubein,** President, High Point
University; Chairman, Great Harvest Company

"*5 Habits to Lead from Your Heart* is the perfect read for busy individuals who can benefit from slowing down, reflecting on their lives, and asking if they are really getting what they want."

~**Patricia Fripp,** CSP, CPAE,
Past President, National Speakers Association

"*The 7 Habits of Highly Effective People* by Stephen R. Covey is a classic in the field. Johnny Covey's new book, *5 Habits to Lead from Your Heart,* continues the tradition. Johnny teaches us that leadership of self and others is not just about technique; it's also about fire in the belly, passion, courage, being proactive, getting out in front, leading by example. He reminds us that the 'think and feel' of the 'inner game' is as important, if not more so, than the outward game of 'doing'. We forget these lessons at our peril."

~**Ted Prince**, Ph.D.,
CEO, Perth Leadership Institute

"*5 Habits to Lead from Your Heart* is an invitation to consciously and courageously create positive change in our lives. Like a good mentor, Covey asks the deep probing questions that challenge us to explore future possibilities and make sound choices. His playbook, head-to-heart approach, and personal stories are sure to inspire and motivate change."

~**Lois Zachary**, President, Leadership Development
Services and author of *The Mentor's Guide*

"In *5 Habits to Lead from Your Heart*, Johnny Covey clearly and simply outlines the principles and plays for creating positive change—and confirms that it all starts by applying our courage—moving from our head to our heart and taking action to reinvent or restore ourselves."

~**Sandra Ford Walston**, The Courage Expert, author of
COURAGE: The Heart and Spirit of Every Woman,
The COURAGE Difference at Work and *FACE IT!*

"Johnny Covey's *5 Habits to Lead from Your Heart* offers a refreshing and compelling framework that illustrates the power of presence, choice and creation that naturally occurs when you align heart, mind and conscious. Masterfully written, Covey calls on us to be introspectively courageous as he skillfully, yet simply, describes the flux and flow between being in the present moment, understanding the nuances between what *happens to us in life* and our *life experiences* and making purposeful choices for transformation and fulfillment. The ripple effects of these Habits extend well beyond self, home, and work. They are, indeed, the building blocks that shape and inspire change across communities and the world."

~**Michelle Lopes Maldonado,** Chair/President,
Northern Virginia Conscious Business Alliance

"While it's clear that Stephen R. Covey's 7 *Habits* inspired Johnny Covey's 5 *Habits*, this original work expands on the life-altering principle of proactivity in a fresh, creative, next-generation way. The entire head-to-heart concept deeply resonates with me, as the subject is indeed close to my heart."

~**James Mapes,** bestselling author of
Quantum Leap Thinking

"In *5 Habits to Lead from Your Heart,* Johnny Covey recommends that we proactively choose to respond from the Heart (without excluding the Head). He aptly demonstrates how to trust our Heart and provides creative strategies and practical guidelines for thinking, feeling and doing each Heart habit. *5 Habits* is a must read for people wanting to enhance their self-worth and authenticity and build a growth-oriented, meaningful life. Lead from the Heart!"

~**Carole Kanchier,** Ph.D. psychologist and author
of *Questers: Dare to Change Your Job and Life*

"Johnny Covey's *5 Habits to Lead from Your Heart* is a compact, logical guide to improving interpersonal relationships. The 5 Habits—Be Courageous, Be You, Be Present, Be Restored, and Be a Conscious Creator—offer a self-help framework that apply whenever and wherever human emotions play a major role. While not directly business-oriented, I discovered several areas I could apply Covey's insights to my work and life."

~**Laura Stack,** President of The Productivity Pro, Inc.
and author of *Execution IS the Strategy*

"*5 Habits to Lead from Your Heart* offers lessons in how to live particularly suited for our era, when so many of us have had to adjust our expectations. After experiencing the worst of our new century's Great Recession, Johnny Covey dug deep into his heart and discovered enduring wisdom that offers balance and meaning in chaotic times. This book is worthy of Stephen R. Covey—high praise, indeed—and it is a great gift."

~**Sally Helgesen**, author of *The Female Vision, The Web of Inclusions and Thriving in 24/7*

"In my work with leaders across multiple countries and cultures, I see common challenges. In *5 Habits to Lead from Your Heart,* Johnny Covey gets to the heart and soul of these issues: Effective leadership of teams and organizations always starts with effective leadership of self."

~**Brenda Bence**, author of *Would YOU Want to Work for YOU?* and *What's Holding YOU Back?*

"Clear, concise and current, the *5 Habits* playbook is a perfect companion and guide as you play the Game of Life, your life. With conscience as your personal internal compass you will discover the courage to be yourself and know the joys of spontaneity. Choose how you think and feel today, in the present moment, and then choose to do something to invent your own principled, purposeful, authentic life—one that affirms yourself and others. With this playbook in hand, trusting your heart as the generative core of who you are, you can look forward to one 'Whoopee' after another."

~**Wan Su**, Founder/Chairman, The Pacific Institute-China

"Some books are irritating in a positive way, and this book for me is one of them. After reading and reflecting on Johnny Covey's *5 Habits*, my heart compass is many degrees closer to true north now. Thank you for your gift and inspiration."

~**Thomas Reichart**, CEO of Reichart Leadership Group; former CEO of FranklinCovey Europe

"This is the one book our generation needs—it's an antidote to our greatest problem: *We have systemically taught our hearts to take a back seat to our heads.* In school we learn to teach our hearts to *fit in*, to not be authentic, but rather to put on masks to gain rewards, to get out of our hearts and *be smart*, to impress others with our mechanized drives to *fit in*, *get ahead*, *measure up*, *obtain more*, *get good grades*, *seek the next promotion*, and *analyze every decision*. We seek the safe path *most traveled*."

"In all this, the head rules. The heart is often ignored, even shouted down, when it tries to tell us vital things we need to know, feel, and do. We consult *experts* rather than rely on our inner wisdom. Even in our closest relationships, we often treat our hearts like children whose role is to be seen, not heard. Johnny's book is a modern-day MBA for the heart, teaching us how to reboot our creativity, initiative, innovation and passion for life and work—how to *get real* and reignite our genuine self. This is not another *outside-in* self-help book; it's the opposite. You'll experience a profound exploration of a place where the heart is a full partner with the head. Beware—this may be alien territory, so use this book as your guide."

~**Oliver DeMille**, *New York Times* bestselling author, founder of Thomas Jefferson Education

5 HABITS

TO LEAD

from YOUR

HEART

Getting Out of Your Head
to Express Your Heart

Johnny Covey
With Ken Shelton

Made for Success
PUBLISHING

Made For Success Publishing
P.O. Box 1775 Issaquah, WA 98027
www.MadeForSuccessPublishing.com

Distributed by Made For Success Publishing
Design by DeeDee Heathman
Illustrations by Cotton McCulloch and Morgan Potter

First Trade Edition: June 2016

Library of Congress Cataloging-in-Publication data
        Covey, Johnny
        5 Habits to Lead from Your Heart: Getting Out of Your Head to Express Your Heart
p.cm.

ISBN: 9781613399026
LCCN: 2016900211

Printed in the United States of America
First Trade Edition: June 2016

Book design by DeeDee Heathman
Illustrations by Cotton McCulloch and Morgan Potter

For further information contact Made For Success Publishing
+14255266480 or email service@madeforsuccess.net

DEDICATION

To **Christine**, who loves and believes in me with all her **HEART.**

To my **Children**, who remind me to play with all my **HEART.**

ACKNOWLEDGEMENTS

When I realized that Ken Shelton (who worked with my great uncle Stephen R. Covey on the 7 Habits and was the editor of Executive Excellence and Personal Excellence) lived near me I asked for an introduction from one of my clients. His first edits proved he was as good as I had hoped. Over the next year I would drive to his home and we would wrestle with what to do next on the book. Some might think it's odd to put your editor on the cover, but Ken's willingness to invest his experience in this book as if it were his own should be acknowledged.

My true love Christine has been my partner in creating the Head-to-Heart framework and putting it into the 5 Habits. You can see her work throughout the book making the stories personal as well as sharing her story by being mentored throughout the book. Her ability to clarify an idea, editing the content for flow and impact was exactly what the book needed. As we each have implemented these principles personally, in our relationship and our family it has been a beautiful co-creation. I am so grateful she has been willing to embark on this journey together.

To my parents who provided me with experience after experience of being in my Heart.

To Bryan and Deedee Heathman. Their vision on what the book was and could become is all I could ever want from a publisher, not to mention their willingness to do the work to get it there.

To Catherine Barrack for her ability to edit from the reader's perspective.

To every previous experience along the way that has brought me to this point.

CONTENTS

FOREWORD

BY STEPHEN M. R. COVEY

My late father, Dr. Stephen R. Covey, made a strong case in his best-selling book *The 7 Habits of Highly Effective People*, for *choosing our response* to the conditions and conditioning of our lives. In fact, this principle, that we are free to choose and are responsible for our choices, is the basis for his first habit, *be proactive*. It also is the foundational principle for all the other habits.

In my book *The Speed of Trust*, I make the case for cultivating relationships of trust in order to accelerate desired outcomes and results. I believe that nothing is as fast as the speed of trust and that nothing is as profitable as the economics of trust. But to sustain relationships of trust with others, we must first begin by *trusting ourselves*. Trust is an inside-out process. For example, we'll have a hard time sustaining trust with others if we don't trust ourselves, because at some point that distrust of self will typically get projected out into our relationships. But with self-trust as our foundation, it becomes far more natural and abundant for us to create and sustain trust in our relationships, teams and organizations.

In this book *5 Habits to Lead from Your Heart*, my cousin, Johnny Covey, has his own unique way of combining these two concepts. He focuses on the proactive behavior of choosing in a way that favors the heart without excluding the head. Learning to trust our heart is the most important thing each of us can do for ourselves, and Johnny shows us how we can do this intentionally. He shows us how we can exercise courage in being who we really are, how we can use our imagination and intelligence to consciously create our experience and how our choices profoundly affect what we think, feel and do.

I've known Johnny his entire life and I know him to be a remarkable, caring, creative person—and a force for good. He's a person who from his early childhood, courageously chose to exercise his proactivity, creativity and authenticity, even when these choices incurred social or financial costs. He models well what he teaches in this book, and because of that, he can serve us well as a mentor in this process of conscious creation.

Johnny can help us move wisely from head to heart. He can help us learn how to be present. He can help us consciously and conscientiously create positive changes in our lives—to more fully express our talents, to realize our potential and to be restored to our real, authentic, best selves.

Johnny uses the metaphor of running, or executing, "plays" as a means of helping us in the process of conscious creation. Having had three sons who each were all-state football quarterbacks in high school, I know the purpose and value of running a well-designed play to get desired outcomes on the field. Similarly, Johnny has given us numerous well-designed plays we can run to help us get desired outcomes in our lives. In fact, I see this book as an extensive playbook for proactive *quarterbacks*—each of us—who seek to lead meaningful, worthwhile lives of purpose and contribution.

So, for our own benefit, I hope we might apply the principles in this book to become more proactive and deliberate in our choices. As this is a book we experience, and not just read, I predict many of us will benefit so much from this that we'll desire to recommend it to others who may also benefit. They will thank us for our thinking of them.

We can experience being restored to our true and best selves by choosing how we think and feel and then doing the plays to exercise our conscience and explore new possibilities. Johnny shows us how to do this in the most intentional way possible—by leading from the heart.

INTRODUCTION

Experiential Playbook
Choose to Experience the Possible

When I first read Stephen R. Covey's book *The 7 Habits of Highly Effective People*, as a teenager I was searching for who I really was. I had a vague sense of what was possible for me, but I had no clue how to reach my potential.

This was the start of 14 years of searching for the answer to this question: *why don't I choose to do what I know?* I've read hundreds of books, attended dozens of conferences and invested over 10,000 hours to create the answer: the *5 Habits to Lead from Your Heart* and the head-to-heart framework. It enables you to create change within your family, company or culture.

Stephen taught us to *be proactive* (habit 1 of his 7 habits) by *choosing our response* to conditions and conditioning. The *5 Habits to Lead from Your Heart* expands on his principle of proactivity. It enables you, regardless of your previous experiences, to not only choose your response, but choose your present experience—creating a world of possibility through conscious creation.

In my first book, *Choose Your Experience*, I expanded on his principle of proactivity to encompass choosing not only your responses to environmental stimuli, but also choosing what you experience as a result. I subtitled this book *Getting Out of Your Head to Express Your Heart* because I tried to capture the essence of the proactive process.

When I first started playing golf, I was told that the only book that I would ever need to read on the sport was Ben Hogan's classic *Five Lessons*, because this book captures the fundamentals as expressed and experienced by a master golfer so well.

Now, in this book, I convert the head-to-heart handbook into a Hogan-like *playbook*, a progressive series of *five habits* that propel your personal and professional development, as well as your business development: 1) be courageous, 2) be you, 3) be present, 4) be restored and 5) be a conscious creator.

My Aim: Facilitate Experiences

My aim here is not to inform and inspire you with examples of my experiences. Rather, as a mentor I hope to facilitate new experiences, enabling you to choose to create change as you go from your head to your heart. I show you how to get into your heart—to enable you, regardless of who you are and what you have experienced in your life, to create new experiences.

I know I have not had your experiences. None of us has identical experiences. For example, consider siblings who grow up under the same roof. Even with the shared environment and common genetics, their experiences are vastly different. While I haven't had your experiences, I can offer to mentor you because I too have had experiences where I've misunderstood my conscience and chosen to go against it. I have felt that pain and used that pain to change.

I can mentor you in the head-to-heart process because I have gone through it myself. Other mentors will come when you are ready. Also, you can use this process to mentor others. We become who we are by learning from our own experience and the experiences of others.

My aim is to help you understand *why you do* what you *do* and how to *choose* wisely. Throughout this book I outline these principles and provide plays that will *change* what you *think, feel* and *do*—if you choose to create change. My intent is not to tell you what to think and feel, but rather to show

4

you a new way of *how* to think and feel, enabling you to consciously create experiences that change what you do.

I will focus first on *principles*, then *practices*. Why?

Principles = Timeless truths that work every time

Truth = Reality based on *principles*

Practices = How people apply *principles*

This process is not meant to be understood all at once. In fact, you will only fully understand it when you *experience* it.

My Personal Experience

While I haven't had your experiences, I have had similar experiences with many of the fluctuations of life.

For example, 10 years ago, my wife and I, as newlyweds, built a $500,000 home. I had started my career investing in properties and was riding high during the 2006-2007 real estate boom. I bought my dream car, a boat and another car to tow the boat. We vacationed in the Caribbean and our HOA provided the pool and tennis courts.

We loved our lives. We were involved in our community. We contributed in meaningful ways to our neighbors. Our marriage relationship was strong. We were fulfilled. Our first two children were born in our dream house. We planned to live there for a few years before selling it at a healthy profit. However, we made the wrong investment choice at the wrong time and we went through foreclosure.

We then moved from house to house to motorhome to house to motorhome to house to house—all within a five-year time span.

I no longer had a booming business, big home, fast cars or an impressive income; in fact, I might be considered a failure by some people.

But here's the thing: as my wife and I were losing everything, we were just as fulfilled. Yes, we were curious how things would work out, but we were still happy. We did not gain fulfillment from owning a nice house, boat or car. In fact, without the pressure of maintaining a certain standard of living, I could see myself more clearly and I learned how to choose my experience, no matter how my circumstance changed: whether I was rich or poor, single or married, father of one child or seven children.

Even now, internally, I continue to feel that I am incredibly successful. In my business I only work one day a week with clients; the rest of the time I think and write. We live in a small split-level home that we rent. We drive cars that we buy with cash—models from the 1990s—and plan on a budget for annual repairs. I earn enough money working one day a week to provide modestly for my family. We have many things and experiences we want and everything we really need.

I tell you this because I am now *choosing* to experience my life, not just doing what others say is best for me. Many people have told me to change, but I feel that this life is what is best now for me and my family. It is how my wife and I want to live. We give up some aspects of other's lives so that we can have some perks that most families don't take advantage of. I am choosing to experience life based on something internal, not external. I go out with my wife twice a week on date nights. My work schedule is flexible and that allows me to be a very hands on dad. We chose to have our children fairly close together, so they need a hands on dad to match their mom. As of June 2016, our children's ages will include newborn, 21 months old, 4 years old, 5 ½ years old, 7 years old, 8 ½ years old, 17 years old and 17 years old (No twins - teenaged foster daughters). Because I'm not working with clients every day, I can split the load of carpool, laundry, dishes and discipline with my wife during the day so that she can play tennis and commit to other projects outside her family. I spend personal time with each of my eight children every day. I spend most of my time thinking and solving problems, which is what I love to do. I am very fulfilled.

This does not mean I am not progressing and seeking more financially. It's just that I am enjoying this stage of my life, not pining over the past or fearing the future. I have dedicated much of my time over the last five years to thinking about and writing this book. Soon I expect to leave this stage, as I switch from writing to scaling—taking what I have developed in this book and giving it life outside of my small circle of influence. I am reinventing myself and my focus, applying these same 5 habits and the head-to-heart process.

An example of a time where I was going through the head-to-heart process is when I was meeting with a mentor of mine at my favorite restaurant. I was eager to tell him about what I would be doing with my life. I could count on one hand the number of people in my life who had the same impact that he had on me. I was so excited to tell him about what I would be doing because I was leaving a business where the only purpose was to make money and joining the industry he was in, which changed people's lives through teaching principles.

The reason for leaving my money-making business was not as noble as it sounds. It was primarily because I had lost everything. That failure changed my thought from making money so I could fulfill my mission, to fulfilling my mission and trusting that the money would come.

As I told him my plan to be a speaker, mentor and business consultant, I could feel something was not right. He was not excited like I thought he would be. He was distant. As I finished explaining my plan I asked him, "What do you think?"

He said, "You will starve."

I was shocked, embarrassed and hurt. Never before had I ever heard anything but encouragement. I defended my position as best I could, yet he did not change his view based on his experience of what it would take to succeed.

The next few days I was frustrated and depressed. I did a lot of exploring what I was experiencing through writing about what happened to get clarity on why he said what he said. It was not because his love for me had changed. It was because he did not believe that *he* could do what I proposed. He was trying to protect me. He got into the industry a traditional way, after putting his time in at a normal job, after completing his undergraduate, graduate and post-graduate degrees.

The courage to explore why it happened, to still believe in myself and to choose for myself was the most courage I have mustered up until that point. It was courageous, not just because of what he said, but because of the hundreds of obstacles I would have to overcome. I was in my mid-twenties with practically no money, no credibility, no content, no mentors. However, my conscience kept telling me to have courage because I knew it was what I was supposed to do.

That meeting was a turning point for me. I had to dig deep and really commit to my path. Yet at the same time, I knew the value of listening to the experience of someone who knew far more about what was ahead of me than I did. I had to figure out what was really going on for me. I had to become present to where I was really at, not just where I wanted to be or where I would end up eventually if I took this path, but to be aware of and present to that moment.

I had so many experiences where I felt like I was doing what I was born to do. This was what I should be doing. I also had many experiences with my mentor believing in me. I was able to separate the lie from the truth. What was so painful was the lie that he did not believe in me, that he was not supporting me, that somehow I was less than what he thought I should be. These were all lies that I had created in my own head. I made my own pain. It hurt so badly because it wasn't true. The truth is that if I chose the path I explained to my mentor, it would be a hard road. The truth is that it would take years to make the money I would need to support my family on that individual business plan.

It is incredibly painful when we believe that something is wrong with us and we are alone. I have had plenty of other experiences where people who did not believe in me told me that what I was doing made no sense. Those experiences gave me feedback to change. Not that what people said was always accurate, but that there may have been something in it that I did not see before.

What it all boils down to is that our experiences either take us to a place of trying to protect ourselves or to progress. It is up to us to choose to use our experiences to progress, to learn from our experiences, to learn from the experiences of others. That can mean following their example or to know that is what you do not want to do.

My guess is that you are presently having experiences where you feel that others think something is wrong with you, and perhaps where *you* actually think something is wrong with you.

If I only…. If they only…?

My guess is that you are presently having, or have had, experiences where you feel alone, where you do not fit in.

I am too… I will never…

What if the problem was only in the way you were *choosing* to experience those things? What if the problem could be solved, even if no one else changes?

The first step to solving a problem is to know *what* the problem is. The second step to solving a problem is to know *how to know* how to solve it. The third step to solving a problem is to put *energy* into solving it.

The reason we keep having the same problems over and over in our lives is because we don't know what the problem is, step one. Yep, I said it. I don't think you know why you are having the problems you are having. It took me years of going against the grain, not believing that the current solution was working, to get to the root problem, which brought about a different solution, step two. I will give you everything you need for steps one and two. Your responsibility is to complete step three and put energy into solving it.

In the next two sections I will outline the problem and the solution. The rest of the book is there to support you in putting your time and energy into choosing your experience.

My Invitation and Challenge

I invite you to learn, apply and share the *5 Habits to Lead from Your Heart* and the head-to-heart principles. Much of this material may seem familiar and foundational—it is. That is why it works. You are already choosing to do it at some level—to choose to create the results you want in your life. After reading this book, you will know *how* to choose to consciously create change, but ultimately you must choose to do it.

Section 1 will lay the foundation to use the head-to-heart framework. Section 2 will use the head-to-heart framework as a tool to have you experience the 5 habits. These 5 habits allow you to lead from your heart and will give you everything you need to know to get out of your head and express your heart. I have put together additional tools and resources for you at ***www.5Habits.me*** so you can keep experiencing the process of going from your head to your heart long after reading the book. It is the best way to take the practices and principles of the book and personally experience them.

The plays at the end of each chapter ask questions and give an example encouraging you to create your own experience. Try the principles for yourself—test them to see if they allow you to choose to be you—your best self—and share them with others.

SECTION 1

Lead from the Heart
Learn to Shift from Head to Heart

"Wherever you go, go with all your heart."

~Confucius

We are born to play the game of life leading from our heart.

From the movie *Jerry McGuire*:

JERRY: All right, I'll tell you why you don't have your ten million dollars. Right now, you are a paycheck player. You play with your head, not your heart. In your personal life, heart. But when you get on the field, it's all about what you didn't get. Who's to blame. Who underthrew the pass. Who's got the contract you don't. Who's not giving you your love. You know what, that is not what inspires people! Shut up! Play the game, play it from your heart.

ROD: No heart?! I'm all heart!

Like Rod, you may think that you are "all heart" and are worth millions more than you are being paid; however, you may be stuck in certain *habits of the head* that hold you back.

Once, you and I were *all heart*. As children, we played at life in the present with a sense of our potential. As we aged, however, we tended to shift out of our heart and into our heads—and then tried to drive forward by looking in the rear-view mirror, back toward the past.

The Root Problem
Being in our Heads

*"For every thousand hacking at the leaves,
there is one striking at the root."*

~Thoreau

The root problem is that we play from the past, from our previous experience and from our head, not leading from our heart. In this book, I try to strike at the root problems you face in life—the things that keep you up at night, the things that have haunted you for years.

Our root problems are not due to lack of information—they are based on what we choose to experience. We tend to think that information alone will solve our problems—that if we only knew what to do, we would do it. However, even when we know what to do, when we have all the information we need, we still have the same problems. In fact, they may get worse! We can solve many *external* problems with information, but resolving *internal* problems requires us to experience something new.

We also accept the idea that when we solve external problems, our internal problems will solve themselves. For example, *when I have enough money, I'll have the security I need to feel at peace. When I lose weight, I'll love my body and find the perfect partner for me. When so-and-so stops doing such-and-such, then I can be happy.*

We all know that solving external problems will not automatically create what we want internally. And yet, we still want external things to create what we want internally. We wish that measurable things—like money, weight and time—could start and sustain intangibles like happiness, peace, love and joy. We know we should work on internal issues; however, since working on them is so immeasurable, it's hard to pinpoint where to start, what to work on or how to get the results we want. So, we look outside ourselves for answers.

If you are like me, you have been looking for answers outside of yourself for years. Some of these external things have helped me to a small degree, but have never given me the complete results I really wanted or needed. Often I received the results that were promised, but they did not translate into what I needed.

Why is this?

The Gap in the Game

We may know the truth of who we are and what we want to do, but often we can't do what we want to do because we're not currently experiencing the truth of who we are. There is a gaping hole, a Grand Canyon gap, between *where we are* and *where we know we should be*.

Like all games, the *game of life* has winning and losing strategies. Your ability to win has everything to do with you and your choices. Yes, there is an element of chance or luck in this game, but you still get to choose what you do and who you become as you play.

I use the word *play* because I think that it best describes what you are doing. You are trying something out, seeing if it works. If it does work, you progress; if it does not, you may regress. You have to keep trying until you figure it out.

We all start life at basically the same place when we are born and then we move to where our family, or team, is. If our parents, or team captains, have been implementing losing strategies, we face a daunting challenge—but it's one that we can overcome when we know what game we are playing: the game of our one and only mortal life.

The game of being popular, rich and famous is a difficult game to win. There are few winners; and even when some people win, they feel the excitement of victory for only a moment. Competition demands constant volleying for position and the prize of first place. There is almost always someone who is ahead of you, and you only feel glimpses of satisfaction because of the temporary nature of first place as everyone is trying their best to beat you.

Where are you playing this game?

Christine: I play this game with other moms. I want to be better, to mother better, to measure up and make it on the pedestal if there are medals being handed out.

This competitive game can never truly be won because the end goal is not to be *your best,* but to be *the best*—to be better than others. Out of necessity, we all play this game to a degree; however, we can play it in unhealthy or healthy ways. Few people disagree that competition and comparison do not bring what we really want in the end, but most of us still play this game.

This game says when I do_____I will feel_____. Christine mothers to the best of her ability so that she feels good about her efforts. Yet what about when her ability changes? Or her responsibilities increase to the point that she cannot maintain her normal standards? Rigid expectations usually result in disappointment. Feelings should not have a foundation of actions because individuals produce so uniquely. Because feelings based on what we do are not sustainable, we stop trying. The reason it does not work is because you are going backwards on the results continuum. If Christine wants to feel good about her mothering efforts, there isn't a checklist long enough for her to feel good. There will always be a way to mess up actions. What you do does not permanently change how you feel. Here is the correct order of the think, feel and do continuum: what you do is a result of how you feel. What you think is what actually changes how you feel. The feelings you have are a result of the thoughts you choose.

Maybe you have had these experiences like I have. Whether the game of comparison is something you struggle with or whether you have unhealthy feelings towards yourself, these experiences are trying to get us to change. As you look at this list, notice the experiences you have unhealthy feeling towards:

✓ My body looking the way I want

✓ My house looking the way I want

✓ My significant other being the way I want

✓ My friends being the way I want

✓ My kids being the way I want

✓ My income being the way I want

✓ My job or business looking the way I want

✓ My bills being the way I want

The experiences where you have unhealthy feelings that paralyze you when you can't move through them, like embarrassment, frustration, anxiety and disgust create a troubling problem. The problem is that you don't think you know what to do. However, rarely do we not know what to do, even if it is just the next step.

✓ Eat more greens

✓ Pick up the living room

✓ Schedule time to talk

✓ Spend more time with a specific friend

✓ Spend more time teaching and less disciplining

✓ Find how I can add more value

✓ Talk to an employee who needs support

✓ Call up and cancel a service I don't use

Even if you were to take the next ten steps on each of these, the result may be that you still feel the same. You still feel you have to do more to feel better.

The root of the problem comes from believing *if I do_____ then I will be_____.*

The reality is that we must experience something different. The game of avoiding painful experiences does not last. The reality is that no matter how successful you are and how much you do, you will still have many experiences that will be very painful.

✓ Death of loved ones

✓ Sickness

✓ Trust being betrayed

✓ Being judged by others

✓ Being misunderstood

✓ Lied to by those you love

An example of this was a particular time when my wife and I had a disagreement. It was a real doozy. I ran my usual play of being hurt and offended. I truly believed and told myself *she is the problem.* I took it so far in my mind that I really believed that, *for my life to be better, she needs to change. Otherwise, I'm stuck here.* Anyone who knows my wife would know how incredible she is. What hurt me was that she was letting me know about something that I could improve upon. Instead of listening to her and trusting her, I spent a lot of time and energy trying to help her see what she needed to do to change. It was very obvious to me what she should do and I could not figure out why she would not just do it. I created a lot of pain for her, with unrealistic expectations and instructing her on how she could change.

Maybe you have been like me and wanted someone else to change in order to solve your problem. The real problem in my situation was that I was not being respectful. I was trying to protect myself by making her wrong. I was not trying to be disrespectful; the problem came from playing a game that did not work.

Shocking Experiment

We often don't see options that are right in front of us, especially if our previous experiences show us that they are *impossible*. Consider the implications of this "shocking experiment."

> In the 1960s, before animals had any protection, rights or representation, researchers would electric shock dogs when conducting experiments. One group of dogs could stop the shocks by pressing a lever. Another group of dogs could press the lever but it would not stop the shocks. So then when they put those dogs in a box where they could escape shock by jumping over a short divide, the dogs that had previously been shocked without relief simply laid down, as if to accept their fate. The dogs that had pressed the lever to stop the first shock jumped over the divide to escape the shocking situation. The dogs that laid down could not be threatened, bribed or shown how to jump over the simple obstacle. They had to physically experience being walked through it. The scientists lifted the legs of the dogs and mimicked the action of step-by-step going over the divider. After two experiences, the dogs could do it on their own. (Seligman and Meir, 1967).

> Seligman, M.E.P.; Maier, S.F. (1967). "Failure to escape traumatic shock". *Journal of Experimental Psychology* 74: 1–9.

The reason we do not change is that we have had experiences over and over that bring us to the belief that those dogs had. We cannot change our experience, so we lay down and accept it. There are usually a few things we are willing to change, but they are external rather than internal. The reason for this is because we are using the part of our brain that is designed to protect us. I refer to this as being *in our head*. In our head, our conscience sends our feelings as messengers, telling us to change. We don't understand the message and try and protect ourselves. If we understand that feelings are actually indicators that we need to change, we can choose to use the part of our brain designed to progress. I refer to this as being *in our heart*. In our heart, our conscience uses our feelings as messengers, telling us to have courage and progress forward. Like the dogs, we can jump up and get out of that box. If we are in our head, we protect ourselves and let the past dictate our future rather than progress by leading from our heart. We keep playing the same game looking for different results, even though the solution can be as simple as jumping over a divide. I want to show you how to jump over the divide in your life. The problem is I can tell you all about it (remember the scientists threatening, bribing and modeling for the dogs), but it will not change anything until *you* experience doing it for yourself.

Rather than closing our heart so we do not get hurt, we need to have courage and choose to change how we experience the same experience from our heart. This new way of playing the game is not easy to learn or master, but it is a lot more fulfilling because we progress rather than repeat the same experiences over and over and over.

You can probably think of experiences you have where no matter what you do, you cannot seem to change. They may even be experiences that others are enacting on you. I am telling you there is another way.

You might have had an experience where you walked away feeling:

✓ Ignored

✓ Unappreciated

✓ Left out

✓ Rejected

✓ Made fun of

✓ Misunderstood

✓ Gossiped about

✓ Judged

- ✓ Unhappy
- ✓ Unwanted

- ✓ Unloved
- ✓ Disrespected

We interpret these feelings to mean that something is wrong with us and that we are alone. What if these experiences weren't what you thought they were? What if the feelings you felt were telling you something different?

In summary, the problem is that we have had experiences where we have chosen to use our head to protect ourselves. We think knowing more or doing more will solve the problem, but in reality we need to choose a new experience by leading from our heart.

The Core Solution
Expressing Your Heart

"When we forget how to love and play, we start to fret, fight and go to war. When we forget to listen to our conscience, we risk doing the unconscionable."
~Ken Shelton

As children, we love to play games because games give us a healthy outlet for our competitive drive and a chance to test ourselves against competitors or against some standard of performance. As adults, we play less and work more to solve problems. But remember, the root problems we face are caused by what we choose to experience—and they can't be solved by working harder and longer. We need to play the game a different way, a better way.

Play the Game a New Way—Your Way

I offer you a chance to play the game of life in a way that is far more challenging and rewarding—the game of *your life, your way*. You were born to play this game. You have yearned to play it well, but perhaps not learned how to play it in healthy ways.

Even though I am now an author, I actually received my college degree in recreation. I studied the science of games. I like this definition of what a game is:

"A game is a problem-solving activity, approached with a playful attitude" (Jesse Schell: game designer, author, professor at *Carnegie Mellon*).

In order to play this game, you must first give up the plays in your current playbook that don't work for you. Yes, they may work for you in one area, but they are not *really* working for you. You might not even know it, but you will be able to choose only what works. This will be hard at first, but over time you will see that winning this game of life is the real win you are looking for.

During this game, with the right plays, you will feel worthy and accepted. And there can be more than one winner! This is the abundant mentality— all who play with a winning strategy can walk away a worthy and accepted winner. It's not like in second grade when the teacher told you that *everyone is a winner* just because no one is supposed to lose.

The feeling of *being worthy* is what it feels like to look into a child's eyes. You know that children are worthy regardless of what they do or do not do. Their *inherent worth* is not based on *doing*, but simply their *being*.

Do you remember feeling this worthy?

Christine: I don't. But I assume my parents felt the same way about me that I feel about my children. I had a great childhood. I guess I can remember feeling worthy in Mrs. Bizzell's kindergarten classroom. She didn't have favorites, rewarded hard work and respect and was kind to everyone.

The feeling of *being accepted* is what you feel when children hand you their drawing. You are not sure what it is, but you are proud of them. You know that this was their best effort—and that is enough. It's all you need and all they need. You accept them for being them.

Do you remember feeling this accepted?

Christine: I remember my softball coach in third grade. I can't even remember her name. But she coached me in kindness and promoted our team connection. She wouldn't let us ostracize or hurt each other. She accepted us all and taught us to accept each other.

We may have lost these feelings of inherent self-worth for ourselves. We can see worth in others, especially in children, but to regain these feelings of self-worth we may need to undo what we have done (or what others have done to us) and restore ourselves to *who we truly are*. The only way to restore ourselves in this way is to listen to our conscience. All the plays that I share with you are designed to show you what you must do to listen to your conscience.

Each of us has different experiences and make different choices about those experiences. It is neither possible nor prudent to instruct you every step of the way to do what you must do to restore yourself. However, *you* can know what to do because *you* have been there every step of the way. You are perfectly equipped to retrace your steps and restore the parts of you that have been left behind.

Plays and Practices

We apply the 5 *habits* through *plays*—specific timely practices based on timeless principles that enable you to *personally experience* the habit.

In sports, a game is made up of many plays that are used to score more points than the opponent. A *playbook* is a plan designed by a coach to produce a result, a win. Plays show you how to move around on the court, going from one spot to the next, both on offense and defense, so that you can execute effectively and win the game.

For example, in the sport of basketball, many coaches use a whiteboard to sketch X's and O's, showing their players how to move on the court. I sketch plays on the court of the head-to-heart framework to help you recognize where you are on the court and how to use the whole court to your advantage. The plays help you achieve both public and private victories.

In basketball, there are five fundamentals: dribble, pass, shoot, rebound and defend. During the game, all ten players on the court are applying these fundamentals to win the game. What makes the game exciting is how they execute these basic skills against their competition.

If you are on offense trying to score, you dribble and either pass or shoot. If you don't have the ball, you maneuver into position so someone will pass the ball to you, or you set a screen so someone else can receive a pass or shoot. On defense, you guard someone to prevent them from scoring, or you rebound the ball to prevent opponents from having a second chance to score.

In life, when we are on offense, we are playing to progress by being courageous. When we are on defense, we are protecting ourselves. Likewise, the *head-to-heart plays* deal with being courageous on offense and changing on defense. When we play from our heart, we are open to courage and change. When we play from our head, we inhibit courage and halt positive change.

Throughout this book I have drawn out some plays for us that have worked for me and others; however, I hope you will also create your own *playbook*—designing plays that enable you to experience new possibilities.

For example, the play called *be present* is recognizing what you are thinking using your head and heart and recognizing what you are feeling using your conscience. When you do this, you can choose a play that enables you to change or be courageous or both.

If you can't automatically do the play, personally experience it and explain the play to others, the play is not yet yours. None of these plays are of any value to you if they are *my* plays—they become valuable only when they belong to *you*. So, pay the price of repetition to make these plays your own. Again, you may understand the play quickly, but to personally experience it automatically you need to feel it over and over by doing it over and over.

You can master the *5 Habits to Lead from Your Heart* by mastering the fundamentals—mapping out plays and executing them. The play framework helps you to see how it looks, where you should be and what you should focus on doing. In basketball, you might watch game tapes so you can see what the plays look like in action. I will help you visualize the play in your mind so it becomes real with mentoring questions.

Finally, you should *execute the plays* over and over until they become natural. In this process, you can experience the play for yourself. The only reason to learn a play is to use it in the game. The game you and I are playing—the game of life—is always going on. Until we master the fundamentals and know how to use the plays, we will keep losing, settling for what we're given, not getting what we want. In fact, without the right playbook, we can never win the game of life.

My basic plays—the *5 Habits to Lead from Your Heart*—are designed to work whatever your skill level in the game. If you are beginning to choose your experience, you'll focus on courage. If you have been choosing your experience and are ready to restore yourself, to live the life you were meant to live, you will continue to work on these plays to master the fundamentals.

This book is like having a personal mentor to help you learn the principles and plays and get in the game. The sacrifice of playing is great. It's hard to be engaged in an intense game, but the sacrifice of only watching, of being a spectator or fan of other players, is even greater. By playing the game of life, you feel the pain of defeat and the joy of triumph. And you will eventually see that every aspect of the game is good for you and that playing the game in your own way is what makes life fun.

This new game plan is being present to the times you are in your head, listening to your conscience and having the courage to change by being in your heart. This is the process of aligning your experiences, whether they be previous, present or possible with your conscience.

As you become aware of your biggest problem—using your head to protect yourself instead of your heart to progress—you next need to outline the steps to reach a new solution.

When something happens to us, we have the opportunity to choose what to do. If we feel threatened, we react with our head. We protect ourselves from feeling bad. The most common ways to avoid feeling bad is to try to make other people do what we want them to do or to do things that distract us from the pain.

When something happens to us and we feel safe, we connect with our heart. We progress forward. We are open to our own potential and the potential of everyone around us. We are able to figure out solutions to our problems.

Your feelings are how you know what to do. Feelings are very important. Your conscience uses your feelings to tell you to make a different choice or to keep going on the choices you have already made.

If we don't understand the messages our feelings give us, they don't serve their correct purpose. They just pile up on top of each other, day after day, month after month, year after year, decade after painful decade. It doesn't feel good to feel bad about ourselves. With the pain of everything that's ever happened to us dragging us down, we can't move forward to where we want to be. The painful feeling is dissolved when we realize what it means.

That is one of the many results of practicing the 5 Habits; You see things as they really are. You aren't paralyzed by the pain of the past. You can use your head and your heart simultaneously in the way they were meant to be used. You don't live in your head, afraid or angry. You live in your heart, progressing and purposeful.

We are in our HEAD when . . .

- ✓ We use our brainstem and cerebellum or base part of our brain

- ✓ We trigger flight-or-fight responses

- ✓ We think that we are alone and feel something is wrong with us

- ✓ We worry about what others think about us

- ✓ We feel wrong when we are disconnected from ourselves

- ✓ We feel alone when we are disconnected from others

- ✓ We feel awkward, uncomfortable and embarrassed

- ✓ We feel inhibited in expressing our best talents and natural gifts

- ✓ We feel insecure, even disposable and dispensable

- ✓ We feel unneeded, unappreciated, unrecognized or unwanted

- ✓ We feel insufficient—that we are never going to be enough

- ✓ We hold back, self-censor, withhold

- ✓ We seek control or seek comfort

- ✓ We become raptors to protect ourselves even when we are not in real danger

When we are in our HEART when . . .

- ✓ We use our neocortex, or right/left brain

- ✓ We use our intelligence and imagination

- ✓ We think, "I am acceptable"

- ✓ We feel our inherent self-worth

- ✓ We feel worthy of having the best in life

- ✓ We feel worthy when we feel valuable, regardless of previous experiences

- ✓ We feel accepted when we feel enough, regardless of previous experiences

- ✓ We lose our inhibitions in a healthy way

- ✓ What we say and do builds us and others up

- ✓ We can drop our masks and be ourselves

- ✓ We creatively express ourselves

- ✓ We may laugh, dance, sing, dream

- ✓ We listen to our conscience

- ✓ We cultivate growth and discipline and experience progress

- ✓ We are not threatened by the imagination and intelligence of others

- ✓ We welcome change, innovation, imagination and improvement

- ✓ We thrive on abundant thinking

- ✓ We sense our potential for greatness

- ✓ We create change within ourselves, teams, schools and organizations

- ✓ We gain the courage to consciously create

Think about the most influential people in history: Gandhi, Martin Luther King Jr., Mother Teresa, Nelson Mandela and others. They were not successful or celebrated because they did not have challenging experiences. They are known because, just like us, they had challenges and yet chose to have the courage to change. Challenging experiences do not go away. The only thing we really need to do is choose to experience life from our heart.

Flow of the head-to-heart Framework

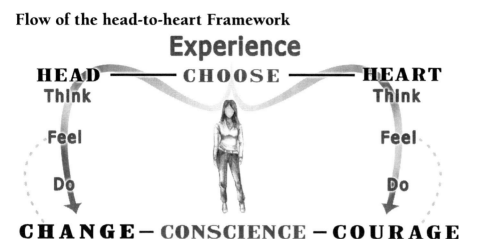

The flow of the arrows will give you a starting point when you use the head-to-heart framework. When we have an experience, we will choose to lead using our head or our heart.

The left side of the diagram is what we experience in our head, what we are thinking, feeling and doing in our head. Our conscience will be sending us a message to change through how we feel. When we recognize that the icky feeling is telling us to change, we can listen to our conscience to change.

The right side of the framework is what we experience in our heart, what we are thinking, feeling and doing in our heart. Our conscience will be sending us a message to have courage through how we feel. Our conscience is telling us to have the courage to continue our experience.

Whenever you recognize you have a feeling that doesn't feel right, it's an opportunity to go from your head, the left side of the diagram, to your heart, the right side of the diagram.

To see the full head-to-heart framework and have the definitions of each word used on it, go to the appendix page 237. If you are someone who likes things to be added a piece at a time, wait until you have read the whole book to use the definitions. If you are someone who wants to see the big picture of what the framework will be at the end, I suggest you turn to page 237.

Using the Head-To-Heart Framework

We are in our head or heart all day, every day. If we are willing to explore and express what we are experiencing, we can then choose to experience what we think, feel and do aligned with our conscience.

The simplest form of using the framework is to recognize when your conscience is sending a message. Explore what you are thinking and express what you are feeling so you can choose a new experience. This is done by asking yourself a question and leading from your heart while listening to your conscience. We listen for the answer through pondering or writing it out, which I call "pen pondering". Doing the pondering process means trusting that the principles of the framework are correct and that your conscience will be your guide. Until you experience it for yourself you may not believe it, but the answers come when you sit and listen.

My son, Johnny, is an animal lover and activist. He watched a close family member remove a stray cat from their home and he was furious. He thought the cat had been mistreated and deserved to stay inside. He came home, insistent that our family member had been cruel and selfish and couldn't possibly be a good person because of this one act.

I took a deep breath, and prepared to show him the other possibilities when Johnny said, "Well, since I don't feel good, I should ask a question. Can you help me think of the questions to ask him?" He nailed it! His strong feelings were telling him that something was wrong with what he was thinking. We came up with these questions. Do you hate cats? Why did you make that poor stray cat leave your house? Do you love me? After finding out the answers to his questions, Johnny could form new thoughts, which were based on reality, and he could feel genuinely better about the person and the situation. Head-to-heart does not mean pretending you don't feel what you really do feel. It means letting your feelings move you to explore what is really going on and expressing those feelings so they don't pile up to affect your future experiences.

Follow Three Ground Rules

The three ground rules to *choosing your experience* are:

1. **Be Respectful** to yourself and to others: follow your conscience in what you think, feel and do. Your conscience tells you what to change and what to have the courage to continue.

2. **Be Your Best:** follow your conscience at your 100%.

3. **Be Present**: experience what you previously would *think, feel* and *do,* experience what you could possibly *think, feel* and *do,* and then choose to experience what you will *think, feel* and *do.*

Now You Know How to Play the Game

I have just outlined new ways of how to play the game of life. What the head-to-heart framework can do is more than what appears on these pages. I have just said that you can choose your experience regardless of what happens to you and this is how you choose, but you may not fully believe it.

Suppose I told you there is this game where each player is represented by a little metal figurine and you make revolutions around a square board as you roll dice to let you know how many spaces to move. You have the chance to buy the spaces you land on and other players get penalized for landing on your space. There are other surprises in the game. You might "go to jail" or receive bonus money for continuing the game. The winner is the last person left with money. Great concept, right?

I know how to play Monopoly and I've just told you the rules and explained to you how to play. I'm certain you agree that I know how to play, but after hearing all of that information, you still would not know how to play, had you never played Monopoly before. Or maybe you've already played and no one explained all of the rules properly to you. You would have to experience it for yourself. When someone has a new game to explain to you, the basics are explainable, but when someone new has never played, you can almost always count on the comment, "Let's just start playing. You'll get it."

If you are interested enough to play the game a different way, learn it by trying it out for yourself and keep reading. Your responsibility is to keep reading and my responsibility is to help you experience the Head-to-Heart framework. Let's just start playing. You'll get it.

Journey of Courage

I offer to be your mentor in this journey of courage because I have personally experienced the head-to-heart process and mentored other people in experiencing these exciting new possibilities. This journey takes the courage to say, *I need help* or *I don't know*. If you are not there yet, consider the possibility that there might be a higher level at which you could play the game of *your life*. What does the end of your life look like, having experienced everything you could possibly want? The difference between now and the end is what I'm committing to help you achieve.

I promise you that when you experience this change for yourself and become a mentor to others, your pain will be replaced with gain and your anguish and panic with acceptance and peace. You will see that all of your struggles have purpose—because they brought you to this point. You can let go of the pain you have felt from previous experiences because you will have what you need on the inside to choose a new experience.

You were born to be yourself. You were meant to have everything you need. I'll help you see that you get exactly what you want in life—a life worth living, along the road less traveled. This road "less traveled" is a challenging one, but one worth traveling. Undeniably, this road means more work for the traveler. Moving toward progress means exploring, expressing and having new experiences. Yet all of the work is worth the sacrifice because of the value the traveler gains. The traveler is transformed. The traveler moves forward with all the confidence in the world because the traveler knows how to get exactly where the traveler wants to be.

Two roads diverged in a wood and I—
I took the one less traveled by,
And that has made all the difference.
~Robert Frost

Choose Your Experience
The Path to Progress

"Four chambers make up the heart of every true leader: competency, intimacy, integrity, and passion."

~Dusty Staub

This section gives you an overview of the principles and practices you need to personally experience the head-to-heart process. My core message is to lead from your heart. We do this as we get out of our head and express our heart. Each of the 5 Habits enables us to do this, which results in our ability to consistently choose our experience:

Habit 1: Be Courageous

Habit 2: Be You

Habit 3: Be Present

Habit 4: Be Restored

Habit 5: Be a Conscious Creator

The first four habits focus on the mental and emotional work of thinking and feeling. You focus on what you think and feel by doing the work to *be you*. Habit 5 focuses on the physical work of doing—of being you and doing something—of consciously creating something.

The only way to make something a habit is by repetition—to do it over and over until it is what you naturally experience.

Each principle can be learned in multiple layers of understanding. And each habit builds upon the principles of the last habit. It is a developmental sequence. We may be at different levels within different habits. It is not requisite to master habit 1, be courageous, in order to move on to habit 2, be you. Yet without the ability to be courageous at some level, you will not be able to truly be you.

Because the 5 *Habits to Lead from Your Heart* are connected and built on each other, there is a lot of overlap. Habit 3, be present, is explained again in less detail in habit 4, be restored, because it's interconnected. The first step of being restored is being present. In this way, each habit can be used on its own without reading all of the previous habits. For some, this may feel repetitive. It is, and that is how we learn: by repetition. If, by the end of the book, you are able to explain each habit and the principles behind each habit, then I would know that it was repeated sufficiently enough so that you can remember it and use it in your everyday experience.

Principles and Practices

Principles are timeless truths; *practices* suggest how to apply them. True principles don't change. Our understanding of them may change, but the principles do not change.

You will probably agree with all of the principles embedded in the 5 *habits*. The challenge is making them part of what you think and feel so what you do is based upon them.

Principles have far more depth and breadth than practices. A practice is a specific way to apply a principle. There are multiple ways to apply principles. Principles explain the *what*. Practices explain the *how*. You may understand these principles mentally, but you can't understand them completely because each time you feel something, you add to those previous feelings.

Since there is no end to the ways or number of experiences we can feel, we won't ever fully understand these principles. Understanding one principle mentally and emotionally enhances our ability to understand other principles because we can make more connections. Learning a principle or practice is easy, but understanding only comes through *personal experience*—and experience always comes at a price.

The low-hanging fruit of learning is a blessing and a curse: a *blessing* because it is easy to harvest, hold and consume—we eat the reward with little effort; a *curse* because soon after the easy-to-reach fruit is gone, we must expend more effort to gain the same reward. In effect, we must climb high in the tree to find the most delicious fruit. Over time, our ability to know where to go to find fruit, and how to quickly pick the fruit, expands. We know the climb will be worth it, but harvesting the fruit is a skill we still need to develop.

As you go through the 5 *habits*, first pick the low-hanging fruit; when it is gone, start climbing. Make connections with these principles and the practices you currently use.

Are you willing to get to the roots? Are you willing to take what you know and then to create consciously, *on purpose*, not by accident, those experiences that will give you what you really want and need in life? Are you willing to experience it for yourself? If you keep reading and do what I ask, I can promise that you will.

What Is a Habit?

For the purposes of this book, I define *habit* as **a predictable experience of thinking, feeling and behaving (doing)**. Likewise, a *heart habit* is a predictable experience of thinking, feeling and doing based on principles from the heart.

How do we acquire habits? We form *habits* when we choose something so many times that it becomes what we naturally think, feel and do. The first habits we choose as children are based on what those around us choose. In order to fit in with our family or team, we pick up their habits. They seem natural for us because we are so familiar with them. We naturally mimic what we see others around us doing. In this way, parents model much habitual behavior—how and what we eat, what we do with our free time, how we treat each other and what we say.

These can be healthy or unhealthy habits. We may not distinguish between them at first because we presume one or the other is the only option for us. We follow the path of those who raise us. Even if we see that the habit causes us pain, we are likely to keep the habit because it serves a purpose. Changing a habit can alienate us from those who taught us the habit. So, we tend to keep doing what we are taught in the way we are taught.

What are your unhealthy habits costing you?

Christine: My unhealthy habits are costing me friend-
ship, connection and happiness.

If a habit protects us by keeping us alive emotionally or physically, we will keep doing it. The alternative—being vulnerable—seems too risky and painful. Since we have not personally experienced another way of life, we may not see that there is one. The ability to see a new possibility comes primarily from observing the experience of others. Unless we deeply understand what they think, feel and do to choose differently, we find it hard to make the change. Moving from observation to execution is a difficult step. Just having information is insufficient—we must experience the difference for ourselves.

The process of choosing your own experience is the same, regardless of the experience. Besides learning from someone else's experience, you can choose to blend it with your own experience. Learning the process takes time, since there are many levels of experiencing it. So, be patient with yourself. Where you are now is where you are—just take the next step.

We each have the ability to choose our experience, but we need to nurture it. We need to grow in each of the 5 habits to produce and harvest the fruit of our experiences.

Are you willing to be patient with the process?

Christine: I am willing to be patient. I think it will actually help me in my relationships, which is what I really want to improve on.

Do vs. Be

Habits are formed by shifting how we think and feel over and over, so that we act (do) out of habit. I focus on being (what we think and feel) because what you are constantly *doing* is a result of who you are consistently *being.*

This shift enables us to focus on what we can choose rather than on what we want. When we have experiences that align how we think and feel with what we want to do, we can easily do it. Usually we need to experience being who we need to *be* in order to do what we need to *do.* We need to choose a new way of thinking and feeling over and over to do something new.

Your conscience will tell you what to do if you listen. It communicates with you through your feelings. It sends feelings that you must learn to decipher in order to be who you really are. It helps you examine your thoughts and feelings, to learn from experience (yours and others), to choose your experience and to consciously create from potential.

For decades, you have been choosing your present experience, so don't expect your life to change overnight or feel disappointed if *more of the same* is what you want to choose. You may think that you're failing or that this makeover is not working fast enough. Or, you might think that this is hard work and you are in this for the long run.

All it takes is one new thought to change what you experience. Celebrate every time you choose a new experience. As you do, you will stay invested in the process until it becomes part of your life. It becomes a part of you that you recognize because it's always been part of you.

This is not *my* process—it is *our* process. We've all been doing it for years whether it has been in healthy or unhealthy ways. I'll point out to you the ways that you are already doing it. I hope that you will make this process your own and mentor others to do the same.

I am just *one messenger* who is teaching other messengers to listen to *the messenger*—the conscience: the greatest gift each of us has been given. And no matter how much we have gone against it in the past, we can experience a restoration of it.

> **Have you ever had an experience where you felt you were restored?**
>
> *Christine: I feel restored when I am outside. I love my bare feet touching the grass. It reminds me of when I was little and would run around with fewer cares in the world than today.*

These habits outline how to use your conscience as a compass. The best way to use your *conscience compass* is by personally experiencing using it through plays.

Development via Progress and Experience

My progressive development format is captured in the *head-to-heart framework,* which is used to explain how to choose our experience by following our conscience. The two primary paths of development are *progress* and *experience.*

3 P's of Progress: Previous, Present and Possible. The top of the head-to-heart framework outlines the *3 P's of progress.* As you personally experience the *5 Habits to Lead from Your Heart,* you will progress by reflecting on your previous experience—what you used to think, feel and do—then recognizing your present experience and choosing to experience what you will think, feel and do to create a new possibility.

3 Phases of Experience: Think, Feel and Do. Our conscience influences what we experience—what we think, feel and do.

Think is receiving information—what we need to learn or know and why it's important.

Feel is making that information personal so we can experience how it feels. We can memorize that feeling so that we can recognize it and trust it and make it part of our habit. We can learn to recognize our feelings and accurately interpret what they mean. Our feelings are the most personal things we can share with others. And the deepest connection we can have is to feel something together—not just verbally describe a feeling to someone else. Although others are not with you physically, they can feel what you feel—and you can feel what they feel. This emotional empathy enables you to make their experience your own. Even when you have not had the same experience, you can experience their feelings vicariously.

Do is a natural result of what you think and feel. The key to doing something new is not to force it but to *change how you think and feel about it.* Most information is geared toward convincing you to change what you are doing, pleading a case as to why what you are doing is wrong and figuring out the best way possible to do it. We focus so much on changing what we do, but you can more easily change what you do when you *think and feel differently about it.*

As you go from a previous way of experiencing something (the old way of thinking, feeling and doing) to a possible way of experiencing something (a new way of thinking, feeling and doing) you are likely following promptings from your conscience.

I don't presume to tell you what to do because I don't know what you should do. I don't know what you are thinking and feeling. I don't know what you have experienced; hence, anything I prescribe as the specific solution would be off. However, I can give you a principle-based playbook that works. You don't need to know the specifics of what to do—the principles enable you to listen to your conscience so that you come out a winner, every single time.

Pyramid of Experiential Learning

As seen on the *learning pyramid* below, or *cone of experience*, how we actually learn best in life is inverse to how we typically prioritize and practice learning activities in homes, schools and workplaces.

CHOOSE Your Experience

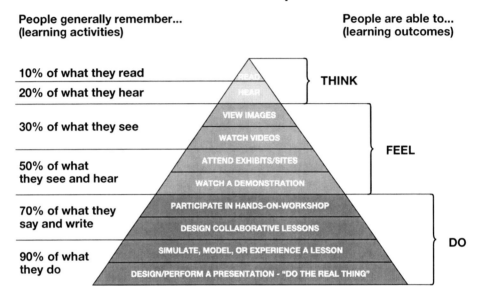

People generally remember...
(learning activities)

People are able to...
(learning outcomes)

10% of what they read
20% of what they hear
} THINK

30% of what they see

50% of what they see and hear
} FEEL

70% of what they say and write

90% of what they do
} DO

READ
HEAR
VIEW IMAGES
WATCH VIDEOS
ATTEND EXHIBITS/SITES
WATCH A DEMONSTRATION
PARTICIPATE IN HANDS-ON-WORKSHOP
DESIGN COLLABORATIVE LESSONS
SIMULATE, MODEL, OR EXPERIENCE A LESSON
DESIGN/PERFORM A PRESENTATION - "DO THE REAL THING"

Dale's Cone of Experience

As you see here, we remember the least in the ways our society teaches the most. Our children are sitting in classrooms, reading and listening to lectures about information. The greatest retention is showcased on the bottom of the cone: experience. We see that we learn most and best by doing, by having experiences, especially by proactively choosing our experiences.

Plays for Thinking, Feeling and Doing Differently

You can read this book, or you can experience it. To help you experience this book, I give you **plays** that enable you and others to go from your head to your heart. The delivery of the head-to-heart experience comes from my **think, feel and do** method. Each habit uses information to change how you think and stories and examples to change how you feel. You then have a chance to do something to make it your own.

Mentoring questions and plays enable you to record the new way you think, feel and do and then share what you will think, feel and do with others using the **1,2,3** method:

1. Mentor yourself by exploring and expressing your experience.

2. Mentor one other person about what you discovered.

3. Implement it in a group of 3 or more. This could be in a work, family or social setting. This is where you choose a new experience.

Another way to say that is 1) teach yourself, 2) teach another person and 3) teach a group of 3 or more people.

The first step of the self-mentoring process is listening to your conscience and you will see an improvement in your ability to choose your experience. If you want to see more improvement in your ability to choose your experience, make it a daily habit. I'm always pleasantly surprised at how much better I feel when I have committed myself to exploring, expressing and consistently choosing my experience. Christine and I are always reporting to each other, celebrating over our choices. *This, this and this happened but it didn't hurt like it has before because of this, this and this.* After we can mentor ourselves, we are then able to mentor another person and eventually implement it within a group.

To hear the experiences and examples of others going through this process, go to **www.5Habits.me** to experience it for yourself.

SECTION 2

5 Habits to Lead from Your Heart
They Form a Development Sequence

"There are two distinct sorts of ideas—those that proceed from the head and those that emanate from the heart."

~Alexandre Dumas, *The Count of Monte Cristo*

HABIT 1

Be Courageous
It's the Universal Requirement

"There's only one requirement of any of us, and that is to be courageous. Because courage defines all other human behavior. And, I believe—because I've done a little of this myself—that pretending to be courageous is just as good as the real thing."
~David Letterman

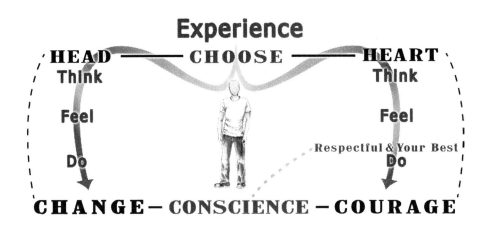

Being Courageous is choosing your experience.

The arrows show the two pathways available when we have an experience. We can choose what we experience using our head or using our heart. What we experience is what we think, feel and do.

The dotted paths show the connections within the framework. In our head, we have the opportunity to choose to change. In our heart, we have the opportunity to choose to have courage. When you lead from your heart, you follow your conscience to be respectful and be your best.

Habit 1 uses the first phase of the head-to-heart framework as shown above.

In habit 1, we establish *courage* as the foundational principle and habit of the heart. Courage in response to our conscience, triggers progression.

Being courageous is a daily experience if we are to live in our heart. When we have experiences that don't fit where we or others think they should, that is a common place we need courage. One of these experiences for my wife and me was when we decided to become foster parents. At the time we had four children, ages 5, 3, 2 and 7 months. So, understandably, it seemed like a crazy thing to do. Yet we felt strongly about it as we were listening to our conscience.

We had people very close to us disagree with our decision. They had either personal experiences or heard from others' experiences and felt like it was not a good decision for our children. They were trying to protect us. They even questioned our motives because they felt so strongly about it. It took a lot of courage for Christine and me to talk through what they were experiencing, separating it from what we were experiencing.

It has ended up being an amazing experience for our family to expand to include children from other families. Our children have greatly benefitted from having older sisters. We have had so much progress because of it. As parents, we have had to really intentionally choose how we would parent teenagers who had not been raised in our family culture.

The most magnificent acts of courage have come from our teenage daughters. Their courage to stand up for themselves and choose a different experience than what they were raised in is incredible. Choosing to have courage to change is not easy and is very painful.

Some of the most courageous things they do would not be noticed by anyone except themselves: choosing to walk away when a relationship is one-sided, choosing to talk to a stranger, choosing to forgive. These are the silent, private victories that have brought powerful change to our teenagers.

You may not see the ways you are being courageous, just as our girls do not always recognize fully how courageous they are being. Each night in our home, we try to highlight one family member. We start with a game where they get to act out some sort of animal (think of the zoo we must live in with nine people, average age of thirteen!). We all try to guess what they will choose. Then the rest of the family members take the opportunity to share with that individual the characteristics and attributes that we love about them. Finally, they get to share what they love about themselves. Almost every time, I tell the teenaged girls how proud of them I am and how courageous they are. I do this because every week they are continually choosing *courage*.

CHAPTER 1

Children of Courage
You Are Worthy and Accepted

"As a man thinketh in his heart, so is he."

~James Allen

All you need is one visit to the playground to observe the courage of children. The contrast would be even more relevant if, when you went to the playground, you imagined that each of the children were actually adults. Imagine the bravery, we would even consider it audacity, of one adult walking up to another and just starting to play beside them without saying a word. Or introducing themselves and picking up an extra shovel and starting to dig. Or screaming at the top of our lungs to defend an injustice. All children start out courageous, without the hesitancies and social norms we create as we grow older. We were all once children—and we still are children to someone. We all came into existence in the same way: tiny, frail, vulnerable—and perfect. Have you ever held a newborn baby? Smelled a newborn baby? We all started out so innocent and unblemished. And then life happens. We begin to have a choice.

I love my children. I know I was born to be a father—their father. I know that at times they won't be doing what they should be doing, and that is part of the learning experience in life.

My children are constantly on my mind as I see them grow. I see wonderful experiences ahead for them, as well as challenges. This does not alarm me or make me panic because I know what to do—not that I know what to do for each child in each experience—but I know what to do as a father to show them how to *choose for themselves* and how to listen to their conscience because of the experiences I have had and questions I have asked.

For many years, I have sought to answer such questions as... *Why do I know what to do and yet I do not do it? How do I change? Is what I am experiencing normal? Why would I feel this way? Why am I not doing my best?*

Such questions prompted me to more questions. Questions are good things. I hope that you have questioning minds and that you aren't scared when you don't know the answers. Some questions have answers that come to you easily, intuitively. But the answer to some of the best questions is: *I don't know.* When you get this answer, you open your mind to new possibilities, new ways of doing things that are better than the old ways.

Please don't be afraid of thinking that *you don't know.* Not knowing does not mean that you are stuck, stupid or wrong. Not knowing means that you're ready to learn new things. Being able to say that *I don't know* will serve you well for the rest of your life.

Above all, learn *how to choose.* Knowing how to *choose your experience* will guide you throughout your life because it will lead you to your conscience, which is all you need to experience what you want and everything you deserve to experience in this life.

We learn in two ways: from others' experiences and from our own experience. Sometimes we want to experience something before we decide that we don't want it in our lives. That can be painful. Sometimes we keep experiencing pain until we learn the lesson that we need to learn. Other times we watch others go through painful experiences and we are persuaded to choose differently. We don't need to experience the same thing for ourselves.

We need to learn in both ways. If you have any regret in your life you need to know that there is always a way back to feeling worthy and accepted. You can choose to listen to your conscience and change at any time, and it will be as if you had not chosen otherwise.

Worthy and Accepted

There is nothing that makes one human being more important or more valuable or more necessary than another. I believe we all have this common potential within us with the chance to contribute incredibly to the world around us. No human has more purpose than another based on nationality, culture, creed or gender. We all start the same way. Why should our value change simply because time has passed? We discriminate based on accomplishment, pedigree, skin tone and personality. What if we lived, accepting others around us, acknowledging the worth of every individual?

I believe that we are all worthy of being respected. When we are being respectful we accept our best effort and the best efforts of others. Accepting others includes being willing to see that there are reasons we all choose what we choose. We all have had experiences that bring us to where we are. When we stand in front of a person, we must remember that every person comes with experiences that have brought them to that point. Our efforts are acceptable because we are all trying our best with what we have to work with. We often think otherwise when we have experiences that leave us feeling wrong and alone.

Once my wife, Christine, had an experience that left her feeling bad about herself. She asked a boy on a date to a Sadie Hawkins dance. The boy said *no*, and his rejection made her feel that she wasn't good enough, pretty enough or fun enough to be with, and that she would *never* have a boyfriend. Of course, I think she is wonderful, gorgeous and fun to be with. And she has a great boyfriend now—me! But between those years of feeling rejected, she had to separate lies from the truth in order to live the life she lives today.

The truth is that *we are all worthy* inherently because we all come from the same place, the same way. We all have equal footing with our common beginning. Everyone is born perfectly as babies. The lie is that some people are better than others because of what they produce, where they are from or who their parents are. Whether we believe we are better or not, it's all false. It's a lie.

At the core of who you are, you are worthy. Where you are is acceptable if you are trying your best. Yes, it's hard to understand someone else's best effort because we have not walked in their shoes. But if we could slip into their life experiences and sense everything that ever happened to them, we would understand them and accept their efforts because we would see everything that went into them.

Our conscience begs us to accept the truth of our worth. The reason we feel so terrible when we choose to not follow our conscience is because we go against what is true. We start living the lie that we are either less or more than others, going against what we know to be true.

If we feel alone or lost and don't know where to go or what to do, our brain tells us that we are in danger and need to find help fast. We become worried and afraid. These feelings come to us to prompt us to seek safety or to find our way out, to make a change so we are never lost again.

Feeling that something is wrong and that you are alone is not telling you that you *are* wrong and alone. Your conscience is telling you to change in order to have a different experience.

Hole in My Shirt

Once I went to school wearing a shirt with a hole in it. I loved the shirt so much that I wanted to wear it regardless of the hole. At school, I started to worry if others would see the hole in my shirt and what they might think— that I had no money or that my parents didn't care what I looked like. I was embarrassed to have someone think that I was poor. So, the rest of the day I focused on not letting people see the hole in my shirt. I no longer loved this shirt. In fact, the shirt was now a source of pain. Of course, in reality, I had caused myself the pain with what I was thinking. No one even noticed the hole in my shirt or said anything about it to me or treated me differently because of it. And yet, I still had a painful day.

Have you ever been in your head, yet no one ever noticed?

Christine: I freak out when I'm late to something and I'm trying to get everything out of my way – children, spouse, traffic – so that I can get there on time. But it rarely is the emergency I make it.

When we have a thought that goes against the truth of who we are, we feel horrible, even if we are the only one who knows about it. It does not matter if it's true. The pain is telling us to open our eyes, to examine what's happening and make a change so the pain doesn't become part of our daily experience. Anything that goes against the core of who we really are will feel horrible until we rediscover the truth.

Fortunately, with my shirt I was able to put on a new shirt and have a new start. I saw that the shirt was not part of who I am—that I was able to take it off.

Mend the Experience

When we see a life experience not as representing who we actually are, but rather as something we are experiencing, we can hold onto those experiences or shake them off and even repair them.

The best scenario is to repair the experience, since we can't change what happened to us. I could not pretend that I didn't have a hole in my shirt. But I could change what I was *thinking* about the hole in my shirt. The pain in my day was telling me to change, to see it a different way, to repair the hole while still keeping my shirt.

When you believe, as I truly do, that *any experience we have had can be mended*, then you will do what it takes to mend the experience. Our experiences can be mended because we are all inherently worthy and accepted and when we listen to our conscience we can feel this way once more. This is how I feel about my children: *you are worthy and accepted, and any feeling you have that tells you otherwise is a chance for you to change how you're thinking about yourself.*

Often we don't mend our experiences because we don't know how or we don't believe we deserve it—we are not in enough pain yet to make a change.

I can show you how to change, but to believe you are worth it, the effort is up to you. You must choose either to believe me (and the experiences of others I share with you) or to operate only off of the things that you've gone through.

Remember the two ways of learning: your experience or through the experiences of others? At first your previous experiences will feel more real than the experiences I share with you because the feelings that go with your own experiences are very strong. You may agree with what I say most of the time, but you may not have the feelings for yourself to support your belief, yet.

The only way to create lasting change is through experience. You will have to test what I say and experience it yourself. This won't be easy, but it will be worth it. You will need to take courage from the experiences of others and follow them.

The hardest part is the pain you will feel. To mend your experiences, you need to experience painful feelings. This is not a spectator sport, but rather a real-life practice—one where you experience some of the pain in order to mend the wound.

Painful Bike Experience

When I was a boy, I loved to ride my bike. Once I was riding it on some gravel and slipped and crashed on the road. My arm was scraped and one knee was covered with gravel. The rock was actually embedded in my knee. Wailing, I went home to my mom. She is very sensitive to her kids when they are in pain; in fact, she feels the pain with us.

She knew how painful it was for me because I had a high pain threshold (at least that was what she told me). I soaked my knee in the tub, but the smaller pieces of gravel did not come out. When mom told me she needed to scrub the gravel out, I was terrified.

As she scrubbed my knee, I did everything I could to hold still. She hugged and kissed me and told me how brave I was. It was so painful that I just wanted to leave the gravel in my knee. But my mother knew it would only get worse and infected if we left it in. Eventually, the knee did heal and I have no scars or sign it even happened, only a faint memory of the pain.

> **Can you think of a painful experience that has changed you where the pain is now faint?**
>
> *Christine: I wanted so badly to find my soul mate. It took me much longer than all my friends. I was the third wheel for years. I thought I was unlovable. It was so painful. Now, I have my true love and it's hard to remember ever being single.*

Our body teaches us to care for ourselves and to stop the pain we feel. In a sense, the *feeling of pain is a gift*. When we get hurt, we may not want this gift of pain, but without it we would not know when or what to change. We would not know how to heal without the pain.

Scrub Our Thoughts

To mend this way of thinking, we may need to metaphorically *scrub our thoughts*. This is a painful process. If the thought has festered and never been scrubbed, it is even harder. We need to bring up the previous experiences and thoughts and scrub the infection. It is not just a one-incident scrub, but one that has built up over time. If you know that what you are doing will clean and heal the wound, you can choose to go through the pain, knowing that in the end you will feel better again. There is a purpose to your pain. Learn what that pain can teach you. Eventually, the mind will be clean—you will no longer feel the pain and will know what to do next time.

As you experience this book, you may feel as if I am scrubbing an open wound. You can choose to let me do this or not. I ask that you trust me—I have gone through the process of cleaning my own wound while others looked out for me. I offer you the same experience.

Challenging Experiences

Some of my children—ages newborn to teen—have already had very challenging experiences. Our teenagers left their birth parents because of unhealthy experiences.

We all have different experiences, but at the core we have the same human value. We are all human beings on earth. We are of worth, regardless of our experience. We express our value in different ways. In that way, we are each unique, and uniqueness is what makes you yourself.

When you know for yourself that you are not your experience, you can *choose your experience*. When you can separate yourself from what's happening, you can choose how you experience what happens. If you are what you have experienced, then you are stuck within that experience. Fortunately, your experiences are just there to assist you in discovering who you are. With your conscience as your guide and the map I am giving to you, I have no doubt you will come to the conclusion that you are worthy and accepted.

It Is Time for You to Be You

I often use the word *experience*, so let me tell you more about what I mean. **What we experience is what we think, feel and do**. Most of the time we focus on *do* because that is the end result. It's the fruit of our work. But I will focus first on what we *think* and *feel*. The reason is that what we think and feel will determine what we do. The good news is that we get to choose what we think, which affects how we feel and determines what we do.

For example, if you think that green food tastes bad, you might feel angry if you are told to eat it anyway. If you think that green food is healthy energy, you will feel excited to eat it. I actually told my children that broccoli was a tree and they would become giants by eating those trees. I even showed them a stuffed toy that I called Mr. Broccoli. So, their thoughts about green food affected their feelings, which affected their actions. To eat or not to eat—that was the question, and it became their choice.

One of the most rewarding experiences you can have is to choose what you think for yourself. To understand what thoughts you are choosing and see if they are working for you.

Much of what you and I experience comes from our environment. We tend to think, feel and do what those around us think, feel and do. However, we control our *circle of influence*. You can choose to let certain people and things into this circle of influence and learn from their experiences. As you do this, you repeat an important pattern—listening to your conscience so that you can be *true* to yourself, over and over, until it becomes a permanent part of your way of thinking.

You may choose to continue your current behavior or change. It takes courage to change, but you can do it. Where you are is where you are, so just take the next step. You have everything you need to take the next step, and you deserve it. You are worthy. You have already been doing this process, and it is the reason you are here—so let's get to it.

PLAY 1: POSSIBLE COURAGE

Where could you possibly have courage that you currently do not? Maybe it's in your marriage. Maybe it's in your business.

What is that *one thought* that comes to mind that you would like to change? If you can't think of the thought, think of the action you would like to change and try to find the thought that goes with why you are choosing that action.

What would that do for you? What would that be like?

Write out on the diagram the thought you could possibly have courage to change.

Experience

CHOOSE ——— HEART
Think

_____
_____
_____
_____
_____
_____

CONSCIENCE – COURAGE

Join the **www.5Habits.me** community to see what others are experiencing for Play 1.

CHAPTER 2

Journey of Courage
You Were Born to Be Courageous

"He has the right to criticize who has the heart to help."
~Abraham Lincoln

Our conscience sends us messages and prompts us to choose to stop doing what we are doing or to continue doing what we are doing. *Choosing courage* is more than just a nice tagline for a motivational speech—it is a way of thinking that can be developed when we understand what we are feeling. This leads us to do what we believed we never could do.

In the fifteenth century, a young French peasant girl, Joan of Arc, was called to save her country from its enemies. Something about her endeared her to her followers and caused them to have a respect—almost reverence—for what she was trying to do. Her sacred sword, her consecrated banner and her belief in her mission helped her to defeat opposing armies.

Courage is transferable. If you have a strong sense of mission, clear purpose and absolute conviction, people will follow you. By displaying her courage, Joan of Arc motivated the French army and gave them courage and confidence. However, she, like other leaders, had her share of cynics and critics. Once she said to one of her generals, "I will lead the men over the wall."

The general said, "Not a man will follow you."

Joan of Arc replied, "I won't be looking back to see if they're following me."

The word *courage* comes from Latin *cor* and French *coer*, "The heart as a source of feelings, spirit, confidence; strength of mind to carry on in spite of danger or difficulty; bravery, valor, heroism; greatness of spirit in facing danger or difficulty; strength in overcoming fear; bold and daring defiance of danger; bravery in fighting an enemy and boldness in accepting risk or sacrifice for a noble or generous purpose" (Webster's Dictionary).

Courage is often called "the mother of all virtues" because when we lose courage, we literally lose heart—and therefore lose life. Daily in our lives we are called upon to be courageous.

Fortunately, courage is part of you. You were born to be courageous. You need to recognize how you are being courageous so you can continue to be courageous and expand on it. Think about your courage. How do you overcome your fear? When do you defy danger? What do you sacrifice for a noble purpose? You may not be courageous, as in jumping into a burning building to save a child, but courageous, as in willing to make the hard choices.

Where have you been courageous?

Christine: I'm courageous when I get out of bed, willing to do everything on my list, even though I have so much left over from yesterday. Courage is just moving forward and not giving up.

My most courageous decision was to discover my message. I was 17 years old. After reading Stephen R. Covey's book *7 Habits of Highly Effective People*, I knew what I wanted to do: to share truths that enabled others to experience positive change in their lives. At the time, I could not even put my mission into words, nor did I have a clue as to what I would do or how I would do it. It was more of a feeling than a clear way of thinking. Because of that choice, and many others, I am now writing this book.

Our Choices Matter

Choices are what matter. The real courage we have is not in *what we do* but in *how we think and feel*. This is why it is so challenging to follow the examples of others. All we see is what they do—the result of who they choose to be and how they choose to think and feel. We see the internal battles only to a limited degree. They provide an example, but they do not give us an experience. We only change when we choose to have a different experience.

An example from someone may encourage us to choose, but example alone will not do it for us. We have to choose to get in the game—to go from spectator on the sidelines to player on the court. The only way to get off the bench is to have the courage to start where we are—not where we think we are or where we think we should be.

Life is painful when we lack courage. Without courage, we are not playing from our heart. Our average day filled with courage may not appear impressive or extraordinary to outsiders—unless they know what to look for.

Day Filled with Courage

You know you have a day filled with courage when you: feel what you are experiencing, are open to what your feelings are telling you and share how you feel with others. This is true courage—living in your heart. To jump in front of a train, to risk physical safety to save a child is to be brave; however, to risk our heart to connect with the heart of another is true courage.

> **Where could you be courageous and share how you feel?**
>
> *Christine: I could be courageous by reconnecting with a family member. We are not as close as we used to be. I think now I want the closeness that she was offering years ago when I didn't want it. And now our timing is off and we are both so busy.*

Many things we do can help us avoid feeling—food, alcohol, drugs or technological disconnection. These things may give us a momentary feeling of relief, but they do not give us the feelings we desire. They just numb the feelings we do not want to feel. If I feel bad about myself, I might try to eat in order to feel better. A midnight snack may help me feel better, temporarily, mostly because I'm distracted from the fact that I feel bad about myself. And the food can't keep that feeling from coming back. I become addicted to getting rid of the bad feelings I don't want to feel. So I continue choosing to find ways to keep me from feeling.

To feel what we truly want to feel, we must understand how our feelings work. To understand how our feelings work, we must understand how our brains work. Our brains respond to what we experience. We set up patterns for thinking so our brain knows what to do when something happens. These patterns can keep us alive, but they can also keep us from truly living. To change these patterns we have to believe that we choose the pattern.

We Choose the Internal Experience

We may not get to choose our *external experience*, but we do get to choose our *internal experience*. This is a painful truth because we can no longer blame anyone else for our lack of courage. We no longer can point the finger and place the blame on anyone but ourselves.

The noblest act of courage is threefold: first, acknowledge that what we choose to experience is our personal responsibility; second, to not punish ourselves for it; and third, to do the work to change it. These are truly courageous choices to make.

When we are present to where we are and what to do next, we then see that the most courageous thing to do is to take the next step—to be respectful and forgive others and ourselves, to be our best, giving 100% effort, while letting others do the same, and to stop comparing ourselves to others—to give up the belief that we are more or less than someone.

Through these courageous acts, we allow an *abundant mentality* to govern our way of viewing the world. We see that *there is enough!* There isn't a cap on achievement, good characteristics or qualities in people around us. We need not compete or compare to gain our value, let others gain their value or lose all value. We all need to make comparisons; but, when we use comparison to bring someone up or put another person down, we are not leading from our heart.

We usually use our brain to make choices. The ability to choose is our brain's greatest ability. It is what makes us unique and gives us freedom. Freedom is not a one-time choice, but a daily choice within the mind. We forfeit our freedom of choice when we are stuck within our experiences. We take away our own choices when we limit ourselves with our own expectations or the expectations of others. In reality, we must choose to recognize that we are free to choose, unhindered by tradition or expectation. As we choose, our greatest victories are only known by us since we are the only ones who know what we have chosen—and we are the only ones who can choose otherwise.

When have you changed internally, even if no one else noticed?

Christine: I stopped making it my responsibility if others around me failed.

I let go of that. Looking back, I can see how unhealthy it was, but in the moment I had no idea. A therapist pointed out the codependent relationships in my life. I was so invested in outcomes in other's lives, I would smother and micro-manage because that is where I measured my value. It sounds crazy because it was. Now I know that my value is set. I am worthy regardless of what I or others produce.

PLAY 2: PREVIOUS COURAGE

Where have you previously had courage? Maybe it was in your relationships. Maybe it was pertaining to your health. If you can't narrow down the thought, think of the action you changed and try to find the thought that went with it. What did that change do for you?

Write on the diagram, in the left hand column, your previous thought. On the right hand column write out your courageous thought.

Experience

HEAD ——— **CHOOSE** ——— **HEART**
Think   **Think**

C H A N G E— CONSCIENCE — COURAGE

Join the *www.5Habits.me* community to see what others are experiencing for Play 2.

CHAPTER 3

Courage in Conversation
Exploring One Experience In-depth

"Conversational intelligence is at the heart of any transformation process because it activates the courage to change and reduces resistance and fear."
~Judith E. Glaser

My wife, Christine, and I have the same challenge in our marriage that most couples experience—the challenge that comes from being different. Later in our marriage, Christine told me she truly thought we were the one couple on earth that really was perfect for each other. In our marital bliss, she thought we would never divorce, never disagree, never even have a different opinion! She thought we were so well matched because we were exactly the same. Of course she knows now that the secret to our happy marriage is the way we complement each other. The reason we are perfect for each other is we are different—complete polar opposites.

This is **an illustration of the most important way to have courage** in our relationship. Christine is motivated by producing; I am motivated by peace. She creates as a playmaker, organizer and project manager. I create as an artist, thinker and researcher. Since we think and feel differently, we often do the complete opposite of what the other would do. We have a similar language, but we do things very differently, even when we seek the same end result.

The issues that arise, whether it be taking care of our kids or working on our business, are significant. They give us a chance to choose courage. It takes courage to want to understand what the other person is thinking and feeling. It takes courage because often what we are thinking and feeling is that the other person is the problem and that he or she should change. It takes courage to look inward to recognize that *I am the problem*. What I am thinking and feeling is because of what I am choosing. It takes courage to choose a new possibility.

When we were first married, we wanted to have a child. After two years, we were finally holding our boy, John, son of John, son of John, son of John, son of Stephen. We have taught our oldest boy to say his lineage that way, and he repeats all the John's and then squeaks out a high pitched, "Stephen!"

We were eager to be parents. We lived in a beautiful home we had built across the street from our best friends. After a few months of waking up every three hours to feed the baby and after he had reached a healthy weight that would enable him to sleep through the night without eating, we decided we could rock him back to sleep and eventually teach him to stay asleep. We were quick to find all the tricks that would work. We created a dilapidated rock in our arms, and he liked the out-of-rhythm bounce and the sound of our shushing in his ear.

After a while, that sound lost its appeal, but we discovered a new soothing sound—the faucet. Running water helped calm him in the middle of the night. One night, Christine walked out into the hallway bathroom and turned on the faucet and rocked baby Johnny in the syncopated rhythm that helped him fall back asleep. I followed her into the hallway and watched in the dark with love as she calmed him down. I put my hand on the small of her back.

She sank to the ground and started crying. She thought I was an intruder, intending harm on her and her baby. Adrenaline started pumping through my veins and I was instantly out of breath from the shock of it all. I called out, "It's me! It's me!"

Deep Relationships

This story is legend in our family. The misunderstanding is always comical when we reenact it for anyone that hasn't heard it yet. It's often a repeat performance for the poor souls who have already heard it. She thought she was in danger, and I was basking in the light of her love for our child.

The punchline of this story is the honest truth: it's me. It's me! It's always me. I'm the problem! I'm the solution! I can't blame my pain, my misfortunes or my problems on anyone else.

> **When were you the problem and did not want to admit it?**
>
> *Christine: Lately I feel like I'm always the problem, but recently I found out some family members were talking about me behind my back. I did not want to admit that I was the one who needed to change. I only wanted them to stop talking about me.*

Just because *it's me* and I'm the problem doesn't mean that I'm lame. It means that I'm courageously looking inward to see what thoughts are causing my pain. I'm courageously changing my thoughts to create peace. Looking inside yourself is the most courageous act possible in a relationship. As I choose to have courage to change or continue, I show that I'm willing to invest in our relationship. And relationship investments usually yield large returns, like a willingness to change on both sides. But one party can't choose for the other person to change. That's why it's always me—always.

The *culture within* a relationship comes from how we choose what we think and feel. Its depth is based on our ability to share what we are thinking and feeling—not just the healthy thoughts and emotions, but to share and work through the painful thoughts and emotions.

It is easy to have a *surface relationship*–a positive relationship that lacks depth. Such superficiality won't assist you in your progression. Life is not plastic. Life is breakable and vulnerable and alive. Without allowing all emotions to help you to progress together, there is no challenge and the relationship gets boring.

Why Bother?

You may ask yourself, *why do I even bother? It is way too painful to have relationships.* The reason we bother is because of challenge and progression. They enable us to listen to our conscience and to have courage. As we have courage, we feel worthy and accepted, which is all we really want. Only relationships can bring us a lasting feeling of being worthy and accepted. Some things can give us that feeling for a moment, but it quickly is gone. When we accomplish something, we then need to take it to the next level to have the same feeling. For example, when shopaholics make a purchase, they feel amazing for a minute, but the thrill soon fades away, prompting them to look for the next thing.

We all know this. We can't experience feeling worthy and accepted by ourselves. And if we can't have these feelings within ourselves, we can't have it within our relationships.

The courage that Christine and I have, to do the hard work, comes from *commitment.* We have committed to raising children together, sharing our lives together. These commitments keep us strong when we don't want to have courage. We have committed to work through whatever challenges come up. Yes, we know very well the reasons couples split up. We have been slapped in the face by those reasons. But we are in this marriage to win this. We are committed.

This is why we are willing to go through the highs and lows with our families. No one else can bring as much joy or pain. We learn from each other, and we learn *on* each other when we make mistakes that affect the other.

Sample Dialogue

I am providing this sample dialogue between Christine and me because it illustrates how you can have courage in a relationship.

It's beyond bedtime. After an hour and a half of Christine and I patiently talking with our seven-year-old son, Johnny boy, I follow him upstairs to see what's taking him so long. I handle the negotiations and trudge back down to our bedroom. Christine can hear the running water.

"Why is he in the shower?"

"He didn't want to go to bed so I told him to shower and then put himself to bed."

"So you just walked away from him?"

"Yes. What was I supposed to do?"

"You were supposed to be the parent and put him to bed!"

"Well, I didn't."

"I know it! You never do. I'll just take care of this myself."

"Well, can we talk about it?"

"No, if I want something done, I just have to do it myself."

She went up and put him to bed. She stomped down the stairs. She put her glasses and her cellphone on the nightstand, laid down on the bed and pulled the covers up over her. I asked her about our nightly routine.

"Do you want to pray?"

"Nope."

That was the end of the talking that night.

Same Dialogue with Thoughts and Feelings

Let's go through this dialogue again and add our thoughts and feelings (in **bold italics**).

"Why is he in the shower?"

Why didn't you take charge? Why does our seven-year-old control you? Now I'm going to have to do it, just like I always do. I feel disappointed, alone and tired.

"He didn't want to go to bed so I told him to shower and then put himself to bed."

Why are you making that face at me? I feel confused and tired.

"So you just walked away from him?"

This is typical! I do the work. I feel angry, disappointed, alone and tired.

"Yes. What was I supposed to do?"

Why does it matter? I feel confused, defensive, alone and tired.

"You were supposed to be the parent and put him to bed!"

You take the easy way out. I feel furious, disappointed, alone and tired.

"Well, I didn't."

Why am I always in trouble? Now you're just being mean. I can't win here. I feel angry, alone and wrong.

"I know it! You never do. I'll just take care of this myself."

Our whole marriage is this way. Things are never going to change. This is why people get divorced. I feel angry and alone.

"Well, can we talk about it?"

We'll resolve this. I can change if you give me a chance. I feel alone.

"No, if I want something done, I just have to do it myself."

Forget this. I feel alone.

Heart-to-heart: Courageous Conversation

We did talk the next morning, after eight hours of sleep (we don't stay up and fight it out). By waiting to have our heart-to-heart, we can respectfully say what we are thinking and feeling out loud instead of trying to read each other's minds and hurting each other's feelings. Even after 10 years of marriage, we haven't developed that mind reading skill. The key words for patterning any conversation are in **bold italics.**

"Can we talk about what happened last night?"

"Yes, I wanted to wait until you were ready."

"Thank you. I was really angry because you didn't step up and handle the situation. I feel like I always have to be the one to do the hard work around here."

"I never want you to feel alone in our parenting."

"Please forgive me for being so sharp to you."

"Of course. I love you. I love our children. I understand the pressure of our responsibilities."

"I wanted to relax tonight, and I thought you were upstairs, taking care of business. So it was really disappointing when you came down and the job wasn't done."

"Of course. *Can I let you know what was going on for me?*"

"Sure."

"I was exhausted after we both stayed up an extra hour and a half talking with Johnny, and I just wanted to come down and be with you. I was sick of arguing with him, and I thought he would take a shower and calm down and go to bed."

"It was so tiring. We were being so patient with him!"

"*I am sorry.* I know it was a short-term solution, but I was so tired of dealing with him."

"Welcome to my world."

"I know, right? But I'm not trying to get out of work."

"But can you see how it looks like you just wanted to be comfortable and that made more work for me? That's frustrating for me."

"I get that. But that is not what I was thinking. I just wanted to take a break from him and be with you. I was thinking that we could work through it and figure something out. This really is just a hard time for us with figuring out how to put kids to bed."

"I know. *What can we figure out for next time?*"

"Alright, I can let you know when I'm having a hard time, and I can ask for help."

"Okay, and I can try to talk about it instead of reacting to what I think you are thinking."

As you can see, we both handled the conversation openly and with respect, sharing our feelings instead of pretending we didn't have them. We were also respectful by asking for permission to share. Sometimes we are not ready for a heart-to-heart conversation. Head-to-head conversations are often just a tug of war for power and control, leaving deep wounds that are hard to heal. Heart-to-heart conversations usually do not happen in the heat of the moment. Another important aspect of this conversation is taking accountability for our disrespectful choices. We each can only mend the mistakes we made. Far too often, we engage in conversations with the sole purpose of assigning accountability to others. Try as we may, apologies are rarely bullied out of others. The last pillar of a good heart-to-heart is taking advantage of the chance to try again and improve in the future. Asking for a solution together is an opportunity to create together. Creation in a relationship is a powerful bond. Our most treasured relationships deserve our time and the energy it takes to be respectful, take accountability and improve.

The top predictor of sustained success is the quality of your relationships, both professional and personal. When we fail to cultivate quality relationships, we see spouses leaving marriages and top talent exiting organizations. The courage to humbly look inward builds relationships. Courageously creating personal change builds stronger families, teams and organizations.

PLAY 3: BE COURAGEOUS

In the heat of the moment, emotions are strong. When you are experiencing a strong emotion, where you feel wrong or alone, disconnected or deterred, unhappy or unfulfilled, explore your thoughts and recognize what you are experiencing (thinking, feeling, doing). If it does not feel good, you know something needs to change. So this play unfolds as you have the courage to question what you are experiencing. First, start with the questions for yourself.

Am I being respectful?

Am I trying my best?

Next, have the courage to see what you are experiencing might not be what is really happening.

Is what I am thinking accurate? Why would I think that? What could the other person be experiencing?

Having courage to look inward and explore your experience makes for an entirely new possibility. As you courageously move from head to heart and open your eyes to new possibilities, you are in position to have more courage and replace the old dysfunctional thoughts. Changing your thoughts will change how you feel and what you do.

An Example of Running this play

Consider the application of this play to my previous conversation with my wife. We both ran this play before we came back together to discuss what was going on. Running this play did not erase the offenses we had committed against each other, but it helped us both come to the conversation, accountable for what we had done and ready to talk honestly about where we had been hurt.

Here is running this play from my wife's perspective.

Christine: Here is what I was experiencing:

Think: My husband is lazy.

Feel: Angry and alone.

Do: I refuse to talk to him about it and just do the work myself.

Ok, am I being respectful?

Well, I certainly feel disrespected. Ok, but it's me. I can see how I was disrespectful because he obviously wanted to talk about it and I refused to talk. I totally refused to engage with him. I wouldn't even pray! I spoke disrespectfully to him. I was yelling and I was being extremely critical.

Alright. Am I trying my best?

Yes. I really was trying my best. And now my best includes being able to calmly think about it and next time I might be able to just ask to talk about it tomorrow instead of fighting it out. Maybe not, but maybe I could.

When I think, *my husband is lazy,* I feel horrible. That does not feel good, so I know something needs to change. I think I have the courage to examine what I'm experiencing to see if that was what was really happening.

Is what I am thinking accurate? Is Johnny lazy? He works hard. He is definitely talented at working smart instead of doing unnecessary work. And I am good at working hard, often doing extra work. He is definitely not lazy just because we work differently.

Why would I think that? I feel alone quickly if Johnny does not help with household responsibilities quickly and accurately, just like I would execute.

What could the other person be experiencing?

Johnny might be frustrated because I am being so demanding, requiring that he do everything my way instead of letting him create his own solutions and being grateful for his contribution to our family.

I am open to a new possibility.

Think: I think my husband loves me. I think we have both been working hard. I think my husband serves me often. I think he wants to contribute if I let him.

Feel: I feel like we are in this together. I feel grateful for having him in my life.

Do: I ask for help when I need it and I can let him know what I expect.

Before we can have a peaceful and loving conversation where both parties are open-minded, accepting responsibility and willing to change, we have to take our feelings for what they are. They are messengers telling us that what we are thinking is not working. So when you feel a strong feeling, before you succumb to your head, examine your thoughts. When the adrenaline is pumping, take the time to confirm that you are living in reality, not in an imagined life-or-death situation. Or go for it—explode into the Incredible Hulk. When you have morphed back into your milder alter ego, reflect on what you were thinking before you smashed everything to pieces. Ask yourself: *what thoughts could be replaced? What could be possible if I would think something different?*

After a night's sleep, Christine examined her thoughts. Here she expresses her feelings.

Christine: I told Johnny to put these examples of our marriage in his book. I am totally okay with being famous for my mistakes because I know I can try again. I know I am trying my best.

So, after a good night's sleep, I was able to separate myself from my feelings of frustration, anger and disappointment. And the experience I had created was based on thinking that Johnny didn't want to help, that he was lazy, that he was satisfied with leaving me with all the hard work, that our marriage load was uneven, that this was how the rest of my life would play out, that I would rather be divorced and alone than married and alone. As irrational as this was, it felt real in that moment.

Those negative thoughts brought some powerful feelings, telling me something was wrong—not with Johnny, not with me, but with my thoughts. I chose to exercise the courage to examine my experience and choose a new experience. What really happens at our house is that Johnny often asks to help, constantly saves me when I'm running late, always supports me when I want a break and my favorite – he always does the dishes. I never do dinner dishes. I also know that my thoughts were not connected to what was really happening because I talked to him about what I was thinking. And he let me know what he was really thinking. The courageous conversation to work it out resulted in clarity, leaving no room for misperceptions.

Courageously examining what I think is happening versus what could be happening can take away pain. It is painful to feel alone. And when I have the courage to look at my thoughts, I can ease the pain. I still have the same feelings, but I can talk about them and work out a solution instead of suffering the rest of my marriage until one day it all explodes. I love experiencing the possibility of this play: be courageous.

You can carry out this play in many ways. Ask a trusted friend to assess your thoughts. Ask a respected person, who knows both parties, for his or her opinion on the situation. Make a list of misperceptions you've had in the past before you go into a situation, so you can identify them if they happen. Note your thoughts after an experience and sift and sort them into what you thought was happening versus what was really going on. Trust that your conscience will help you figure out the truth and recognize when to listen. If you are feeling wrong and alone, you need to examine your thoughts to open up new possibilities and exercise the courage to admit that what you are experiencing might not be what is really happening.

What's an experience you could be courageous and work through?

Write a strong emotion you felt on the left side of the diagram. Write what you were thinking and doing in relationship to that strong emotion. Strong emotions are signals to change or have courage to continue. Check to see if you are following the ground rules.

Am I being respectful?

Am I trying my best?

Check your thoughts.

Is what I am thinking accurate? Why would I think that?

Could you replace your thought on the left side of the diagram with a new thought on the right side of the diagram? What could you possibly feel and do with that new thought?

Write what you could possibly think, feel and do on the right side of the diagram.

Experience

HEAD ———— **CHOOSE** ———— **HEART**

Think   **Think**

_____   _____

Feel   **Feel**

_____   _____

Do   **Do**

_____   _____

CHANGE— CONSCIENCE — COURAGE

Join the *www.5Habits.me* community to see what others are experiencing for Play 3.

HABIT 2

Be You
Your Authentic Self is Always Best

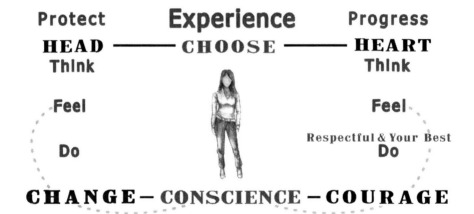

Being You is the process of going from our head, where we protect ourselves to our heart, where we progress.

The dotted paths show us how our conscience sends us messages through our feelings to change when we are in our head or to have courage when we are in our heart.

Habit 2 uses the second phase of the head-to-heart framework as shown above.

In habit 2, you choose to *be you*—once again or for the first time. Habit 2 allows you to be the best version of you as your authentic self—the self that you are in your thoughts, feelings, words and actions.

As I was at the point in my life where I was trying to move on from losing everything in real estate, I tried a lot of businesses to be able to feed my family. The key word is *tried*. I did not invest the time into any of them long enough to get much of a result. I became very frustrated with myself and began to lose my confidence.

When the economy did not turn around, and I was not able to provide for my family, I had to dig deep to find out why I was not doing what I felt I should do. I had built my worth and value upon being an entrepreneur, a great businessman who could make things work. But I could not seem to make *anything* work.

The lower I got, the more I stopped believing I would be able to be an entrepreneur and I started to look at other options. Going back to school for an advanced degree, getting a job somewhere else, looking at multi-level marketing options, etc. I believed that I did not know why I was successful in the first place. I had no idea what made me an entrepreneur. I thought I was a playmaker, but as the market changed, I was not even attempting to make any plays.

One night (actually early morning by then) I was sitting in my unfinished cement basement with a pen, a notebook and a desk. I started to write about what I was good at and what I was not good at. I let go of the internal pressure I had created to be good at the things I thought were important and just became present to where I really was. As I looked at my list of everything I thought an entrepreneur should be, not very much coincided with what my strengths were. Yet I was a great entrepreneur.

I looked at my column of strengths and saw how I used these strengths to be an entrepreneur. I shifted the way I looked at myself and was able to just be myself. I wasn't hung up on what the label of "entrepreneur" or business owner and what they said I should be, and I decided to just be me.

My three-year-old is light years ahead of me. Everyone was planning their costumes this September. We would search on Amazon to find all the right pieces for the costumes that were sure to elicit extra candy on the doorstep. You know the ones I'm talking about. We ordered Iron Man, Maleficent, a puppy, a vampire and Super Mario. After a few weeks of dressing up, Scott came to me and said, "For Halloween, I'm just going to be me." I was impressed. I hope he eventually grasps the magnitude of that statement.

It was a great feeling that night, in my cold, unfinished basement, to decide to just be me.

It was that night that I designed the first draft of the *how to consciously create* exercise. I share the final draft with you in chapter 6. It was then that I started the path of being a mentor and a consultant because I knew that was what I was good at.

CHAPTER 4

Conscience Compass
Follow Your Conscience

"Conscience is a man's compass."

~Vincent Van Gogh

I n this chapter, we will learn to see the human conscience as the universal compass. Our conscience lets us know when we need to change the way we are thinking. Our conscience tells us to change using our feelings.

Feelings and thoughts are interconnected. When we think something that goes against the truth that we are worthy and accepted, we feel sick. This feeling is a red flag, telling us to examine our thinking. This bad feeling is telling us that there is another way.

Too often, we misunderstand our feelings. We feel sick and think there is something wrong with us instead of something being wrong with our thoughts. Our thoughts need to change. Our principles need never change. When we recognize our feelings as messengers to change, we can understand what we are experiencing and choose a new experience.

Conscience Compass

A *compass* is an instrument used for navigation and orientation that shows direction relative to the geographic *cardinal directions* or *points*.

Just as we can map out our physical world, we can map out and progress in our social, mental and emotional world by using our conscience as a compass. Your conscience knows what the next best step is in your progression. It knows where you have previously been, where you presently are and what is possible. Just like a compass gives us direction, our conscience points us toward the right path. It rarely spells out exactly what to do, but it gives us directions of where to go—either to have courage and continue the course or to have the courage to change.

Most of us use our *conscience compass* daily whether we recognize it or not. We know it is important, and we have had many experiences with it. Yet we have never taken the time to understand how to use it. What we experience and our ultimate destination rely on it, yet we do not know how to use it because we have never been shown how and then experienced using it for ourselves. It is much easier to be handed a map and some tools if you can follow directions on how to use them.

Using our conscience compass is the first step. The next step is creating our own map that shows us where we previously have been and what we have experienced. This helps us to recognize the tools we have and abilities we need to develop. This is a lot of work. It's easier to wing it and hope you make it, which works at times, but keeps us from making our own map.

My purpose is not to give you many maps, which are principle based practices, or tools, but to enable you to use your conscience compass to make your own map and discover your own tools through personal experience.

We can learn to make our own map or just set up camp where we are. We can say to ourselves, *this is where I want to be. I like living in the desert struggling to survive.* We then believe, *this is my only option. We grew up in the desert, and we will die in the desert.* We can't see that a fertile valley lies just a few miles away.

Feelings Are Messengers

To help us understand what we are experiencing, our conscience uses our feelings as messengers. Our feelings constantly give us messages to either change or have the courage to continue and endure. If we let our conscience guide us, we will know when to change and when to have courage. We will understand when to change what we think, allowing us to change how we feel and what we do.

We feel *pain* when our conscience tells us that something needs to change. Whether it is because we need to stop doing something that hurts us and others or because someone else is doing something to us or others that our conscience knows should not be happening. Our job is to recognize what we are feeling and seek to understand what the message is. Our job is to change when we know what our conscience is telling us.

Do you know what it feels like for you when you listen to your conscience? Are you aware of what you think when you listen to your conscience? Most of us are not. It is not something we tend to consider. It's a natural process that we don't examine extensively because it happens subconsciously all the time. Our conscience is sending us messages all day long. We may not recognize these messages or recognize they come from our conscience.

Think of the parallel processes going on simultaneously in your body. All day long your body is sending you messages: *I'm tired, feed me, that tastes good, that feels good, stretch me out, I need a break*, etc. We hear the loud messages—the **urgent** and **important** messages come through loud and clear. We can miss the *important but not urgent*, messages entirely unless we focus on hearing the softer, subtler ones, because they don't scream for our attention. The subtle messages provide us with guidance and protection before the emergency ever arrives: *stretch your back before it gets too stiff. Grab something substantial to eat before you get lightheaded.*

Likewise, your conscience sends you many soft messages first, before it gets loud. The messages instruct you to do your best and accept where you are before you attack full force. The messages beg you to feed yourself truth about someone else before you lose your head and yell at them. Don't worry if you are not good at listening to your conscience like you are with your body. You need to figure out how to get out of *emergency mode* and into *preparation mode,* where you proactively prepare instead of reactively respond.

Heeding *important but not urgent* messages and promptings makes for a peaceful life. *Important and urgent* will definitely show up in your life. You can't escape those items, but they need not control you. You can develop this proactive skill over time.

When we understand our conscience, we will know when to have courage with what we think, allowing us to feel and do what we choose. When we understand that everything we experience enables us to choose to go from our head, which is how we have previously protected ourselves, to our heart, which is how we could possibly progress, we access the power to change. This empowers us to have the courage to consciously create change. We no longer are held hostage by our experiences. We no longer choose to be in our heart only when others are in their hearts. We choose to be in our heart, regardless of what we experience.

Our conscience sends messages through our feelings. When you check in, your conscience will tell you to either change what you are thinking or doing or have courage to continue with what you are thinking or doing. It is not always clear which specific thought to change or to have courage to keep, and that is why we need to drill down to the specifics.

When we can't identify the feeling or thought that is connected to the action we take, it's hard to change our behavior. The behavior can change, but all behavior starts with a thought. If you can't identify and change the thought, the behavior remains the same.

Change is difficult. During change, we often feel that we are wrong and alone. We avoid the *change* feelings more than the *courage* feelings because of feeling wrong and alone. Usually feelings that communicate change can be identified. They are strong, often painful, and we feel poorly about ourselves. We misinterpret the meaning of those feelings. Something is not wrong with us or with others, something is wrong with our thought. Feelings of courage probably happen more often without us even noticing. They are easy to miss if we are not paying attention, often peaceful, and we feel satisfied with the results we are getting.

Our conscience sends us two feelings—*change* or *have courage*—and we get to find out which feelings go with which thoughts. Your conscience never attacks you, only tells you that what you are thinking is unhealthy for your progression.

> **Who would you be if you saw your feelings as messengers and followed those messages?**
>
> *Christine: I would be free. I would not feel bad for needing to change.*

We often resist change because our head detects a threat, goes into survival mode and tries to protect us. We may understand what to do in our heart (using our intelligence and imagination) and yet not do it.

The head-to-heart process boils down to being present—simply understanding what our head and heart are telling us, and then choosing the next step. When we do this, we move forward. We progress. It is not harder or easier than that.

When we are present, we can ask ourselves questions and know what to do. We are not bound by what our head or heart says. We can listen to our conscience, the internal compass that knows where to go and what to do. Having a conscience is like having a mentor who never leaves your side. Working as your own personal mentor, your conscience not only understands you, but also comprehends the world around you and can see what you cannot see.

So don't get so caught up in executing the plays of the head-to-heart process that you forget to ask your conscience questions and to listen for the answers. If you can't hear answers, you are too focused on listening to your head or heart. Go through the whole process of hearing what the head and heart have to say, then asking your conscience questions until you can discern what is best for you to do.

I suspect that you are already doing this every day to some degree. As you learn to distinguish between your head, heart and conscience, and as you detect the different purposes of these three voices, you can better understand what you are experiencing. You may ask yourself: *what are the three most important things for me to do today?*

In response to this question, your head will likely be focused on your survival, comfort and security, and supply an answer that is *urgent and important* and leads to short-term success. Your heart will likely be focused on your progress or growth, and supply an answer that is *important but not urgent* and leads to long-term success. Your conscience may tell you to rest, to call someone or to forgive yourself or someone else.

We are listening to all three voices—head, heart and conscience—all of the time, and our ability to understand them enables us to choose wisely which one to focus on.

Either Change or Have Courage

Your conscience can heal you if you will let it. The first step in healing is to understand what your conscience is telling you through your feelings. When you understand that it is telling you to change or have courage to continue, you can then choose to do something different.

Your conscience may tell you to change what you are experiencing. This change could be to make different choices, to have healthier experiences, to stay away from someone who is hurting you, to stop hurting someone else, to stop hurting yourself....

The thoughts we have about these experiences influence what we feel. If some people say hurtful things about us, we feel pain. Our conscience tells us to stay away from them. If we say hurtful things about someone else, we feel pain. Our conscience tells us to stop doing that.

The pain you inflict on another person inflicts pain back on you. If you say or think something hurtful about yourself, you feel pain. Your conscience tells you that either what you are experiencing is unhealthy and you can change and stop doing it, or what you are experiencing is healthy and to have the courage to keep doing it.

Your conscience will not tell you that *others need to change*. That is the job of *their* conscience. You can only change yourself. You may support others in changing, but the first change must come from within yourself.

> **What would it be like to only focus on changing you?**
>
> *Christine: It could be less exhausting, not thinking of all the other things I want people to change about themselves. And it could be scary to only think about changing myself.*

Being accountable for what you experience is difficult—there is no one to blame. Yes, you may rightfully say, "But they really did hurt me. What they did is vile and no person should have that experience. They are doing horrible things."

The fact that your conscience is telling you to change does not change whether these things are true or not—it just changes what you do about them.

You do not get to choose whether what your conscience tells you is healthy or unhealthy. You get to choose to *consciously create* by changing so that you have healthier experiences.

For instance, if someone were to be verbally abusive to you, your conscience would let you know it is unhealthy and to stay away from that person, regardless of whether you know you can choose to change or not. Your conscience sends you messengers—feelings of pain when you believe what they are saying. You may logically know what they are saying is not true, but unless you recognize it is not true, what they say will be part of your thinking. When you absolutely know for yourself that what they are saying is not true and feel that, then you take the reins of your life. Others cannot control you—the words are meaningless.

You have the ability to feel (at least in part) what others feel, but you do not need to make it your own feelings. You can separate those feelings instead of getting tangled up in someone else's experience. The thoughts and emotions of others are their thoughts and emotions. You get to choose which ones you experience. That is true conscious creation—when you choose for yourself. You can choose your own experience, regardless of the experiences of those around you.

When we use our heart and feel worthy and accepted, we can separate ourselves from our choices and allow ourselves to change. Our conscience wants us to change because it knows who we truly are—that we are worthy and accepted—and when we go against that truth, its job is to tell us to change and make different choices.

The reason the *5 Habits to Lead from Your Heart* are needed is simple: **we have forgotten how to listen to our conscience.** We have not always had this problem. As children, we experienced life without the filters that we build up with experience. Some filters support us, others suffocate us. The problem is knowing which ones are which.

Just as your journey to get where you are today has been challenging, so will this journey be. To stay on the path you are on is challenging because of the pain you feel from not listening to your conscience. The pain you will feel as you restore yourself to listen to your conscience will be challenging because you have to open some old wounds in order to heal.

When we open old wounds, we feel the pain, but in the end, we are healed. The pain has a purpose and it has an end. So, what will you choose? Will you choose to restore the real you by joining a new team with a new goal, or will you keep playing the same way that you've always played the game?

This may be the most important choice you will ever make. It is not a single choice, but a series that affects you and those around you. The reason you may choose to restore the real you is because you associate pain with gain. The experience may be painful because your conscience is telling you to change. If you believe that you are broken, you will stop this process because no one likes to be told they are broken over and over again. But if you believe that the play you are running is broken and needs fixing, you will endure the pain.

If you break your arm, *you are not broken*—only your arm is broken. Yes, you are limited in what you can do with a broken arm, but you are not your arm. The arm is a part of you—that is all—and it will naturally heal, if you will let it.

When we do not follow our conscience, we feel broken. That feeling is telling us to change or fix something. The pain is not a judgment of who we are, rather our way to judge what we should or should not think and do. The pain we feel is just a messenger helping us to be healthy. If we listen to the pain, we can adjust what we need in order to allow our body to do what it needs to do to heal. After doing what we can, we can trust our body to do the rest.

Whether you use your *conscience compass* or not is up to you. I encourage you to join forces with others who are on this journey and look for mentors who will support you along this path. Whether you succeed or not comes down to you. You choose your experience, whether you like it or not. I hope that you choose with courage what you experience.

Our conscience is governed by principles just like everything else in our world. It is in alignment just like natural laws we would all agree to. We have spent a lot of time, money and energy seeking to understand natural laws, yet very little trying to understand our conscience and how it works.

I believe this is in part because we do not believe it can be understood. We do not believe that there is the same level of order to it. We do not see our emotions as messengers from our conscience and that the messages make any sense. Yet I believe that the head-to-heart framework can be used to understand what we are experiencing. We can actually track what we experience and understand how what we think affects the messages our conscience sends and those thoughts and feelings determine what we do.

We have placed emotions into their own category. We have looked to the brain or mind as producing our thoughts, yet our emotions are something we don't understand. They are labeled "good" or "bad", but how to do anything with them is a mystery. I believe the next breakthroughs in science will not come from understanding our brain or mind, but our conscience.

It is an operating system like any of the others we have in the body. We have a system to protect us from physical pain such as the nervous system. The lymph system is to protect us from toxins and sickness. The system of our conscience is no different and can be understood.

Now we have a framework to start this journey. My hope is that others in their field of expertise will see this as a tool within their expertise. I am not a traditional researcher who forms test groups and gathers data. I have been proving it works on an individual or small group level. One of my greatest desires is that others will expand upon the understanding of our conscience from a researching perspective and that people will share their personal experiences using the head to heart framework.

The word conscience comes from the latin verb *conscire,* meaning to know. This science of knowing our self is our greatest personal discovery.

PLAY 4: FOLLOW YOUR CONSCIENCE

When we receive a message from our conscience, we want to make a conscious decision about what to do with that message. This play puts a pause button in the middle of what we are experiencing. So instead of wishing we had rewind buttons for all the words and actions we can't take back, we recognize the fact that we do have a pause button. We can create space. We no longer react because we have a choice.

Write out your choices. Select an example experience and write what you would normally think, feel and do from your head in the left hand column. Then in the right column, write what you could think, feel and do from your heart. With your options clearly outlined, you can choose what you think, feel and do—it is up to you.

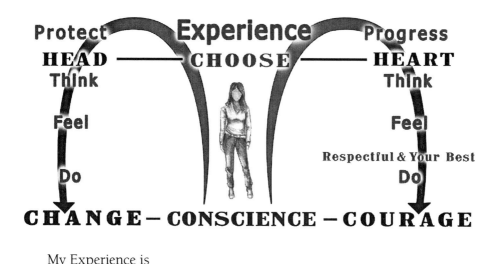

CHANGE – CONSCIENCE – COURAGE

My Experience is _____

In My HEAD...   **In My HEART, I Could Possibly...**

I Think _____   I Think _____

_____   _____

I Feel _____   I Feel _____

_____   _____

I Do _____   I Do _____

_____   _____

Something happens to you (an experience)—you form a thought about it and your conscience sends you a feeling about what you are thinking. Find out why your conscience sent you that feeling. Pause here to decide if you are being instructed to change or have courage to continue. Next, identify what you could possibly think, feel and do. Then, and only then, choose your action.

Join the *www.5Habits.me* community to see what others are experiencing for Play 4.

CHAPTER 5

I Choose to Be Me
My Own Head-to-Heart Story

"A good heart is better than all the heads in the world."
~Robert Bulwer-Lytton

I f all day, every day, your conscience is telling you to change or to have courage, then you will have many opportunities to choose to *be you*. The most courageous choices you make start with the one choice that leads to continuing to choose that path over and over. This is why it is so challenging. It is a daily battle. These daily battles are different for each of us. We have had different experiences, different genetics and come from different cultures. Although we have different experiences, we all face the same basic challenges—to choose to be who we are, to choose to keep moving forward and to choose every day to be in our heart.

My life has been full of experiences going from my head to my heart. I will share a few of them so you can recognize the pattern. I want to share some of my journey of choosing daily to be in my heart and to be myself. My journey is my journey and should not be compared to your journey.

My journey may seem at first like one that does not require much courage. I was born into a home where I felt safe and I could express myself. I wasn't shamed into performing a certain way. My parents afforded me the freedom to choose and learn for myself. I could explore what it meant to be in my heart without being rejected by those I loved most. I did not have to fight for survival. I did not see the world as my enemy, but as my learning and testing ground.

In my story, you will see that all of us are always being challenged in life. The difficulty of unhealthy previous or present experiences can only be removed by making challenging choices that enable you to be healthy. We can be in pain either way, living in unhealthy or healthy ways. I'm hoping you will put a purpose to your pain and accept each challenge to progress forward.

Although I will share challenging experiences from my journey, my most courageous choices are unseen by anyone except myself. These choices constitute the personal, silent victories—quiet moments of choosing to do what I know I should without knowing if it will work. They are moments when people around me told me to stop, yet I knew in my heart to keep going. These are the moments of courage.

I have summarized in my story the head-to-heart framework of what I was thinking, feeling and doing while in my head and then in my heart. None of these experiences happened in one instance. All of them were part of a process that led to having the courage to be myself.

My Story with Head-to-Heart

When I started going to school at age six, I quickly discovered that something was *wrong* . . . with me! "Everybody else gets it," I said to myself. "They get good grades. They can spell and write. And I can't. Something is wrong with me."

I felt like I was alone and not enough—a disgusting feeling at a very young age.

In fifth grade, my teacher couldn't control the class. School was chaos. I started asking myself, "Why try?"

Since I am a peacemaker, I usually choose flight as my response. So I just gave up. My parents were very concerned. They supported me and told me all the right truths, "Johnny, you are smart" and "we accept you as you are."

But I didn't believe them because my *experience* told me that I was dumb and that I was not enough. I reasoned, "I can't do school because I'm dumb."

It made rational sense. So, why try?

Fortunately, my family moved right before I entered the sixth grade. Desperate for me to succeed, my mom went to work at a private school just so I could be admitted there. I had a teacher, Mr. Kennington, who believed in me. He told me the truth, "Well, Johnny, it's true that you can't spell or write well, but you are so creative—your stories are amazing. Just keep writing." He was real with me and told me the truth of what he saw in me.

I started thinking, "Maybe what he says about me is true."

Another teacher, Ms. Mott, believed in me completely and demanded so much from me that I picked up my performance. I started getting better grades and started to think, "Maybe I am smart, in my own way."

A second shift happened socially. I thought of myself as the chubby sidekick to my best friend, who all the girls liked. "Girls just don't like me," I told myself.

But several of my aunts who were in high school kept telling me how handsome I was. Not only were they pretty and popular girls, but in my mind, they were perfect. They could not lie. If they believed what they said about me, maybe it was true. Maybe a girl would like me.

When I started high school, I wanted to reach out to kids who were left out. I felt hesitant, absolutely petrified of what others would think of me. I wondered, "What is this feeling telling me? Is this a bad choice? No, it's not. Just because I feel afraid doesn't mean I shouldn't do it. If I know in my heart that it is right, I need to overcome the feeling of fear and just do it." So, I started reaching out to other students.

At my first high school dance, I noticed that initially nobody was dancing. We were all inhibited or self-conscious to some degree. Finally some kids started dancing—and I joined in! I started dancing like crazy and had the time of my life.

Eventually, I completely let it all out, thinking, "This is who I am. I don't want to be anybody else but me. I choose to be me."

I was no longer worried about what people thought about me. At age 17, I finally felt what it was like to be completely in my heart. I was carefree, in the moment, living in the present.

I read Stephen R. Covey's 7 *Habits of Highly Effective People* and said to myself, "This is what I'm going to do —teach people how to change their lives like this book did for me." I truly believed in my heart that I could be like my great-uncle Stephen. After all, I thought to myself, "I know him; he's just a normal guy." Something inside me knew I could do it.

However, when I started college, I got back into my head again. I said to myself, "Now I have to be professional. I need to do this or do that in order to be successful." I even started to introduce myself as John instead of Johnny because I thought that would somehow be more acceptable. I started thinking, feeling and living in my head. I had to figure out how to get back into my heart again.

This is when I really started discovering the principles of the head-to-heart framework through my experience of restoring myself to my heart.

I eventually got back in my heart, and at age 21 decided to become a real estate investor. I was so in my heart that I believed I could do it—and I did! It took me nine months to do a deal, but I lived off the profit for the next nine months.

When I was going to school and investing in real estate, I thought I was unstoppable. I put together a deal that made my partners and me $1,000,000 from which I personally made over $100,000. I knew I would be rich in no time, and then I figured that I could focus on discovering and sharing my message.

The problem was that the market changed dramatically. I wasn't prepared for the housing market crash in 2008 and I lost everything—my house, my properties—I had to sell it all.

I went back into my head, blaming the market and others. I kept doing what used to work, and it no longer did. I started thinking, feeling and living in my head. I had to figure out how to get back into my heart again. This is when I started developing the head-to-heart framework through my experience of restoring myself to my heart. Living in my head was so painful that I was ready to choose to go back into my heart, ready to let go of my previous experiences and focus on what is now possible.

The market crash forced me to question the timing of my plan: to make a lot of money and then find out my message and share it. I decided to focus on what my heart was telling me instead.

It was not easy to be in my early twenties trying to share my message, but I knew it was what I was supposed to do. I only made a fraction of what I was making before and risked not feeding my family for years. But my wife and I knew this was what we were supposed to do together.

We felt free. We no longer worried about what our house looked like. We went from living in a luxury home to living in our motor home in Wal-Mart parking lots for six months. We no longer did what everyone else did. We were free to choose our own experience. Up to that point, it was the happiest time of our lives.

And it just continues to get better. I am now the father of seven kids with one on the way. Five of them are ages eight and under, and two are our 17 year-old foster daughters. Our foster daughters are in our home because of the choices of their parents. We tell our children, "You are of worth. We accept you as you are. You are not alone. Choose to be you. Choose your experience." Their progression is perfect for them. They are choosing their experiences and changing.

I am not trying to change any of my kids. I simply provide the principle-based head-to-heart framework so they can choose their own life experiences. I want them to know what it feels like to choose what they experience instead of react to what happens to them.

But they have to choose to consciously create change; otherwise, it's not real change. It's control. If I control them, I am manipulating their experience to gain temporary relief from pain—either my pain or their pain.

If I don't want to deal with a four-year-old, who is acting like a four-year-old, I might try to force him to make a different choice. I can use several manipulation tactics to control my child to get immediate results: to stop the tantrum, stop the yelling and stop hitting each other. But if I teach them how to choose—a slow, repetitive process, they will choose eventually. Teaching children how to choose is not a good-looking process. Allowing children to choose rarely looks like something you would want to post on social media. It's not like the annual Christmas letter. You don't write to all of your friends about how biting and potty training is what you've been focused on night and day for the past 365 days. Teaching children to choose means letting children make mistakes and not protecting them from the consequences of their choices. Teaching children how to choose is a painstaking process with beautiful paydays in between long stretches of engaged parenting.

Let's take the four-year-old hitting his sibling. I get down on my hands and knees and look in his eyes and let him know that it is disrespectful to hit. That's breaking the first of three family rules: be respectful, try your best and safety first. I know that he is trying his best and I am, I don't know if happy is the right word, but I'm definitely willing to take the time to teach him that he made a poor choice. So I don't yell at him. I don't shame him into compliance with the family rules. I gently explain to my four-year-old that his brother was hurt by his choice. We get to choose what we want until our choice takes away the freedom of someone else to choose. My three-year-old deserves the freedom to choose to be safe in his own home. *But he took my toy!* Well, that is disrespectful. Your brother should not have done that to you. I will talk to him about taking toys. Right now I want to talk to you about hitting. What's another choice you could have made? I can think of some other ideas, but I want *you* to think of a different choice you could have made. And he usually thinks of something else he could have done. And then I commit him to try that strategy next time instead of hitting. Then he won't get his toys taken away from him if he chooses correctly.

Figuring out a different choice is the first step to realizing that you have a choice! My children are slowly learning that just because something happens doesn't mean that they are required to respond in a certain way. They will grow up into adults that can choose the choices that will best serve their own progress.

It can be exhausting to teach a child to choose. It happens multiple times a day. My four-year-old does not have crystal clear enunciation yet, so it's hard to not crack a smile when I ask, "Why was that a poor choice?" and he replies, "Dis-wee-speck-fo," and hangs his head. The paydays come once in a blue moon when I can almost hear the synapses firing as I watch my four-year-old's toy being taken away from him, but instead of hitting, he comes to me and asks for help. I truly believe that I would rather do the hard work now than have my four-year-old grow up to be a forty-year-old who doesn't respect others. Learning to choose is priceless.

The best part of this for me is that I'm teaching the four-year-old and his experience deeply affects my experience in parenting. But I'm also fulfilling step two of the mentoring process. I'm teaching someone else. I'm solidifying my own education to understand this process and choose my own experiences. I'm not advocating parenthood as the sole avenue for mentoring others, but it certainly provides an excellent opportunity to practice. Mentoring helps you own what you are learning. Everything you are explaining to the four-year-old is personally applicable. I get to choose what I think about my experiences. I get to think of other possible ways I can act. It can be exhausting to do personally, as well, but I have found it to be a lot less painful than reacting from my head. True choice is the ability to consciously create, regardless of what you experience.

What would it be like to accept your children right where they are?

Christine: It would help them not feel like I'm disappointed all the time.

Progress is an inside-out process, driven by choice, not control. It is driven by intelligence and imagination, not fight or flight instincts. It is driven by self-awareness and self-truths, not self-deception. I am now conscious of how to get into my heart and how to show others how to do the same.

This book comes from 14 years of applying these principles. It enables anyone, regardless of where they are and what they have experienced, to go from their head to their heart.

Try the principles for yourself. Test them. See if they enable you to choose to be you. Let's run the following play together and see what happens for you.

PLAY 5: CHOOSE TO BE YOU

In this play, you need to explore and express your thoughts to figure out who you are. Are you representing who you are or who you think others want you to be? Choosing to be yourself means figuring out what you choose and moving forward. There is no mask or camouflage to hide behind, no crowd to impress, no people to please.

Examine the thoughts that you have about yourself. Look to the past to see when you have chosen to be yourself and when you haven't. In the explore part of this play, answer the following questions about yourself.

When do you think you first stopped following what everyone else around you was doing and made a decision for yourself?

What did you think?

How did that feel?

What did you do?

Have you ever had a different opinion from someone close to you?

What did you think?

How did that feel?

What did you do?

If you were giving a seminar to a group of robots to train them how to be you, what would be the title of your speech? What would be some of the important bullet points?

What makes you different from everyone else around you? What is something you have in common with those closest to you?

First, find out who you are and then choose to be you. Do this by asking yourself these questions or one of your own and write your response to see what comes out.

Pick an experience where you have chosen to be yourself or could choose to be yourself. Write out on the diagram what you *think, feel and do* in your head on the left and then what you would *think, feel and do* from your heart on the right side.

Protect	**Experience**	Progress
HEAD ——	**CHOOSE** ——	**HEART**
Think		Think
Feel		Feel
Do		Do

CHANGE — CONSCIENCE — COURAGE

Join the **www.5Habits.me** community to see what others are experiencing for Play 5.

CHAPTER 6

Motives to Consciously Create
Motives Supply Motivation for Mission

*"Authentic leaders align their mission and means behind
their noble motives."*

~Ken Shelton

I n this chapter, we will address several key questions. *What motivates you?
Who or what supplies this motivation? Why do you do what you do? Why do you
do things a certain way?*

Why and Who before What and How

Why and *with whom* we do things should be asked before *what*, *when* and *how*
we do them.

Why ask *why* first? Because *why*, our core motive, determines *what*, the
outcome.

Why ask *who* next? Because who you are and who you choose to work
with can make all the difference in your relationships and results.

Then we should ask *what* and *when* and work out these important details.

Finally, ask *how*, the conscious creation. Don't let the *how* derail the *why* and *what* of your work.

Why aren't more people motivated to perform at their best and highest level? Either because they aren't in touch with their core intrinsic motives and how they consciously create or because their mission, motives and means are out of alignment.

Extrinsic vs. Intrinsic: Motives vs. Motivation

We can be motivated by outside people, forces or influences or *extrinsic motivation*, but we are most likely to move forward toward what matters most to us when we are motivated by internal motives and *intrinsic motivations*.

Extrinsic Motives and Motivation:

Have you ever listened to an inspirational speaker who provided you with information, stories and examples from his or her life in order to help you—and yet you didn't change what you thought, felt or did—you didn't experience anything different afterwards? This is because you were extrinsically motivated. Extrinsic motivation comes from outside sources and systems. Examples of extrinsic motivators include: *people* (parents, coaches, teachers, mentors, managers, leaders, speakers and preachers), *places* (schools, programs, parks, military bases and camps) and *things* (pictures, photos, art, music, speeches, etc...).

Intrinsic Motives and Motivation:

The best way to change is by having an experience and then choosing something different, preferably using intrinsic motivations. This is motivation from the inside-out. Intrinsic motivation is the source of sustaining power—the power to continue doing what you know is right for you in spite of the challenges and opposition. Examples of intrinsic motivators include: dreams, visions, goals, drive, ambition, mission, desire, passions and hobbies.

Understanding Motives

To understand why we do what we do, or our motives, we first need to understand what motivates us, our motivations. Two people can do the same thing but for completely different reasons. For example, one person might clean the house because he highly values cleanliness and order. Another person might clean the house because she has company coming and does not want to be embarrassed. And still another person might clean the house or yard because he wants to gain favor with his wife or impress the neighbors.

Understanding what motivates us enables us to choose to listen to ourselves and do things for our own reasons, rather than doing something because of others. We consciously act instead of being ignorantly acted upon.

Understanding motives also helps us to understand why others do what they do or why they do it the way they do. Such understanding engenders an appreciation for diversity and generates empathy, compassion, tolerance and charity.

Why Don't Others Follow Me?

I do what I do because it just makes sense to me. If it was not the best way to do it, I would change what I do or how I do it. So why would someone else not follow my lead?

I see five reasons—and these are contained in the *5 Habits to Lead from Your Heart*:

1. We have different degrees of courage (habit 1).
2. We are unique and have different motives (habit 2).
3. We are at a different level of progress (habit 3).
4. We have different previous experiences (habit 4).
5. We have different ways we consciously create (habit 5).

Core Motives: Nature or Nurture?

Our *core motives* do not develop in us over time, but rather they are embedded in us when we are born; they are part of our nature. Still, we need to identify them and choose them to supply the motivation we need to exercise courage, to obey our conscience and to be creative.

I use my own children as a case in point. I currently have seven children in my home—five biological kids and two foster daughters. With my five biological kids, I have noticed they are not all the same. Yes, there are similarities because of gender and genetics, but even children of the same gender choose very differently. I have a son, for instance, who will do anything as long as he plays while doing it. If it's a game, he will do his chores. If not, there is nothing to bribe him with. I have a daughter who will do anything to make sure there is peace. Even if she does not get the toy or show she wants. I have a daughter who will do anything for people. She will solve her friend's problems regardless if it helps her. I have a son who has a clear idea and will fight to produce it. He knows what it will take to do it and get it done.

Other motives, our *acquired motives*, can develop in us or be nurtured, and may influence how and what we choose to think, feel and do—depending in part on the situation or culture in which the nurturing takes place.

Elements of Personality

I see our *motives* (both core and acquired) as part of our *personality*.

Personality = Motives + How We Create + What Choices We Make

I define *personality* as our *motives* combined with *how we create* and *what choices we make*. I focus on our motives first because our motives are the key to understanding who we are, our personality and character.

Character: Choices and Behaviors

I define *character* as follows: we are people of *character* when our *choices* are consistent with our *values*, and our *behaviors* are consistent with our *beliefs*. When we choose our experience consistent with our values and beliefs in listening to our conscience, we build character. Strong character ensures consistency in making wise choices and modeling good behaviors.

Different Motives Produce Different Results

We tend to think that one set of motives is better than another, which is not true. It is true that different motives will produce different results, but it is only when we align our motives with results that support those motives that we will ever really be satisfied.

My motives are not your motives. My choices are not your choices. And different motives and choices produce different results.

For example, if your acquired motive is to impress people with your positions or possessions, you may not experience happiness. You may serve and sacrifice for something you think you want, but you remain unfulfilled when you get it. All the work and achievement in the world does not produce a satisfying life if you are not aligned with your core motives. Only by aligning your mission and means with your core motives (who you really are) can you create fulfillment and sustain success.

What It Means to Be Ourselves

What we really want is to *be our best selves*, to feel worthy and accepted for being ourselves. It can be challenging to understand what it means to be ourselves. We often confuse the experiences we have had and choices we have made in the past with who we are. We are *not* our experiences, and yet our experiences are part of who we are.

When we understand what motivates us, we are better able to use both our core and acquired motives to make choices that help us feel worthy and accepted. We feel worthy and accepted when our choices align with our motives and character.

Feeling **worthy** correlates with our sense of worth and worthiness. Feeling **accepted** correlates with our self-esteem and our social relationships. Making choices from core motives helps us feel worthy and accepted.

Four Core Motives: Produce, People, Play and Peace

I believe there are *four primary motives*: *Produce, people, play* and *peace*. We are all motivated by all four motives, and we need to use all four motives at different times throughout our lives. The process of recognizing your motives and embracing them can be challenging because we give up something familiar to create something new. Each motive is a different way in which we feel worthy and accepted. We are all motivated by all four, but generally there is one motive that is our core.

There are healthy and unhealthy ways we use these core motives. When we are using them in a healthy way, we feel worthy and accepted. When we are using them in an unhealthy way, we feel wrong and alone.

Produce

Healthy: If you are a producer, you feel great when you produce impressive results. You love to get things done, to check items off a list, to contribute and be part of great projects.

Unhealthy: If you are a producer, you might not be good at letting others participate if their motives or methods don't align with your way of doing things. You might base your sense of self-worth on what you produce instead of trying to do your best. You might belittle others because they don't produce what you do or the way you do.

You might reach a point where you can't produce enough to meet your expectations of yourself, and your checklists explode.

People

Healthy: If you are a people person, you love to connect with people. The most important things in your life are your relationships. You love sharing what you are feeling and want to know how others are feeling. You treasure deep meaningful relationships.

Unhealthy: If you are a people person, you might get hurt when others don't treat you like you treat them (or the way you want to be treated). You might feel alone, even though you love being with others because you don't feel a deep connection.

Play

Healthy: If you are a playful person, you love to have fun. If it's not fun, why do it? You make activities fun for others as well because you know you can do more if it's fun.

Unhealthy: If you are a playful person, you might be focused on your own experience versus what's best for everyone. You might give up on projects or people because they just don't know how to have fun. The rules of the game are very important to you. You are disappointed often when people don't follow the rules of the game to win when you're following the rules.

Peace

Healthy: If you are a peaceful person, you want to dispel conflict and ensure everyone has what they need. You naturally never want to offend or antagonize anyone.

Unhealthy: If you are a peaceful person, you may find it hard to get a lot done because action may require taking a stand. You are hesitant to have an opinion when it could hurt others' feelings. You can be paralyzed because change can upset the peace in your relationships.

Core Motives Example:

I never understood why my spouse and I were so different. But now, I realize our core motives are completely different. It explains so much! When motivated by *peace* marries motivated by *producing*, it equals lots of learning. So I can't be disappointed because we are both just fulfilling our core motivations. Now that I know about them, I can use it to our advantage.

Determine Your Core Motive

To help you discover your core motives, I invite you to answer some questions, since your answers serve as indicators of what motivates you. You'll be tempted to answer the questions in the way you wish you were or the way that portrays you in the best light. Since you believe that certain results are better than others, you may choose these ideal responses. I encourage you to seek to authentically represent yourself to discover what *really* motivates you, rather than what you have become to get the result you want. In this way, you remain open to discovering what is really motivating you (it may be something other than what you thought was motivating you).

Feel: Core Motive

To determine *your core motive*, label the following sections of statements 1 through 4—1 being the most like you and 4 being the least like you.

_____ a. I feel amazing when I get things done

_____ b. I feel amazing when I connect with people

_____ c. I feel amazing when I express myself

_____ d. I feel amazing when there is no conflict

How You Create: Four Think and Do Archetypes

As you gain clarity on *how you consciously create*, start focusing more on what you're really good at doing—your strengths. If you focus too much on the wrong things, your weaknesses, you get frustrated. If you are focused on how you consciously create, congratulations—you are one of the few. Most of us must consciously shift from those weaknesses to our core strengths and build systems and processes around those strengths so that we keep focused on doing things that we're very good at doing and doing it in the way that we best create.

As you focus on your strengths, you can dramatically improve your life. You create outcomes you most desire. You take the next step toward finishing things you haven't been able to complete previously. Knowing how you consciously create can help you have a rich and fulfilled life. You are free to focus on what you are good at doing—you don't need to feel bad about it. And, it will be something that will help you financially and give you more freedom to be your best self.

Visionaries see the big picture and share the vision. It is all about the big idea. They know that there is an opportunity even if no one else sees it. They want to transform their ideas into reality. You would describe them as brilliant because they think of things that have never been thought of before. They see how to take two completely different ideas and merge them into something better. During the creative process, it is easy for them to not be grounded in the reality of what it will take to execute the vision. They need others around them to actualize the vision. The thought of not working on the big idea and doing the details is not up their alley. A visionary paints the picture for everyone else so another team member can make it happen. Visionaries are open to new ideas and embrace challenging the status quo of thinking. Visionaries need partners who can take over the project once it is up and running. Or they need to recognize when to step down and turn their creation over to someone else. Visionaries pair well with organizers and playmakers.

Thinkers are smart. Thinkers understand complex ideas and they are good at technical skills. They have a vast database of knowledge in things others have no idea about. They make correlations with the way things happen on more of a scientific level than just reasoning. Thinkers are the experts in their fields—people who really understand complex ideas. They have wide knowledge on ideas and concepts of certain subjects. They can be very scientific about the way they approach things. It is useful to have this skill set. These are people who are doctors, researchers, scientists and leaders. If this is you, ask yourself, "How can I be fully utilizing this?" One drawback is that you may go too far into the academics and not enough into getting the action of making stuff happen; or, you get too into the ideas and not much into the necessary steps to take those ideas to fruition. Thinkers need project managers and work well with researchers.

Artists don't necessarily have anything to do with art, but rather everything to do with creating. Artists are continually coming up with new ideas. They think outside the box. They see new possibilities that others do not. They are not limited to their current belief system. Artists are constantly changing and growing. They think in the ideal and focus on the future. Many entrepreneurs create this way, but they rarely realize they are more artist than entrepreneur. Artists are creators. They're always thinking about new ideas, new possibilities, working on *how can we make this work?* They're open to explore new options. They focus on the future and the vision of the long term. They're similar to entrepreneurs in that they like to start things and get things going. If you're an artist, one key to success is following through. It is often difficult for artists to take a project from A to Z. They have the vision, the ideas and the creativity… but how do you take it and move it all the way through the steps so it becomes a reality? Artists need to build a team of people with strengths in organization and execution to help them. They need to be clear with their team members that this is a weakness. It's one of the drawbacks of being so creative—sometimes artists need a little bit of structure.

Researchers know the latest and greatest and where to find it. They know what options are available and the pros and cons of each option. They have a broad base of insight into the next steps. They are fantastic at trying things out, seeing the results and adjusting to create better outcomes. Researchers are very intentional about the choices they make because they have thought them through thoroughly. They save much time and energy by having the facts up front. Researchers go well with thinkers. They really think it through, analyze it and assess what choices will work or not work in a situation. They have all the facts up front and a clear understanding of the consequences. Researchers save us a lot of hassle from going down the wrong paths. Their drawback is being too conceptual versus going out and making things happen. So, if you are a researcher, be sure to try to pair up with playmakers or managers.

Think: Consciously Create using Imagination and Intelligence

Label the following sections of statements 1 through 4—1 being the most like you and 4 being the least like you.

_____ a. I come up with new ideas

_____ b. I understand complex ideas

_____ c. I start new projects from scratch

_____ d. I gather data efficiently

Some of these archetypes below will apply more to you than others. Pay close attention to those that describe how **you** consciously create. With the ones that don't describe how you create, think about how you need to have these people in your life and how you could work together more.

Managers are great at leading a team to accomplish a goal. They are excellent at holding people accountable for what they commit to do. They make sure the system and structure is in place so that everyone in their team can succeed. Managers delegate to others in ways that make it easy for the task to be completed. They can add more value to an organization by helping others succeed than by just focusing on their own success. Managers and project managers have similar skill-sets, but managers deal better with people. Managers delegate, often to the go-to people, the project managers. Managers are very good at helping others succeed. They are team leaders; however, they often need someone, either an entrepreneur or artist, to think outside the box. It's hard for managers to break out of the normal structure of what the current organization is. So, the people to partner with would be people who create like entrepreneurs and artists.

Project managers like multiple projects at a time. They make things happen. Throw a checklist of things to be done in front of them, and they'll perform. They will make sure that things get done in a timely manner. They are very good at being the go-to people. These are people who you want on your team because they say they'll get it done, and it gets done. They figure it out. They know what to do because it's just a matter of getting it done. So, have people on your team who make it happen. If you are a project manager, you need to make sure that you're doing the things that are the most important to get done—don't get distracted by whatever pops up on the to-do list. Project managers tend to do whatever pops up. They need to prioritize activities as they manage multiple projects simultaneously and seek to accomplish everything that is necessary. They are great at understanding what the next steps are and getting them done. When project managers are given a new project, they work it into their system and make it happen. Project managers pair well with managers and artists, filling a valuable spot on the team.

Organizers are amazing at creating processes and systems to stay on task and keep everything in its place. They excel at the small details and plan for everything that could possibly happen. They are efficient and effective at getting things done. They are great at paperwork and maintaining compliance. Organizers are complementary partners to people who are not detail oriented. Organizers are similar to managers. Organizers understand the processes and systems, are great at getting things done and are very good at the small details. They're all about saving some time by creating a better system. These people are very efficient and can improve the organization. Organizers could get too focused on the details and miss the big picture—

the vision of what you are trying to get done. Organizers pair well with entrepreneurs and artists.

Playmakers go out and make the "play" work. They're the closers, finishers and connectors. They know what people and other resources are available to connect with the right people and the right things. They put deals together. They drive a hard bargain. They know their value is making things happen. If you're a playmaker, you have the ability to go out and sell a product or put a deal together. Others want to work with you. They need someone who can help them make it final. However, you may need someone to manage paperwork and details. You have to figure out a way to work with others to take care of those things so that you can focus on what you're great at, which is making it happen. Playmakers figure out how to make it work. They understand the benefits they have to offer and go out and find someone looking for those benefits. They have a knack for working on projects that will work. Because they are out making it happen, playmakers have great insight into what does and does not work. They negotiate effectively because they know the value they bring and convey it in a way that serves all sides. Playmakers pair well with organizers.

Do: Consciously Create

Label the following sections of statements 1 through 4—1 being the most like you and 4 being the least like you.

_____ a. Managing people

_____ b. Managing projects

_____ c. Putting deals together or selling

_____ d. Organizing and creating systems

Don't Label Yourself

Don't think, "Oh, I'm an organizer. That's all I do. Now I feel like I'm a robot. I am going to only focus on organization." Understand that this is something that you're naturally good at. How do you take it and do more with it? What relationships can you build with other people with ways to create? So, don't get too concerned about, "I'm stuck. I don't want to be an organizer. I don't want to be an entrepreneur." There are resources all around you. You have relationship resources to tap into, whether they be with acquaintances, partners, friends or family.

Also, look at what your top two are. If your top way you create is *artist*, and your second is a *visionary*, it doesn't mean you're not a visionary. Usually there's a lot of overlap. We all create in all 4 ways but now you know the top 2 ways you are motivated to consciously create.

Using the head-to-heart framework, you can align your motive and how you consciously create with what you experience. The 5 habits give you the courage to choose your experience and restore those *real you* experiences. Part of this exercise is recognizing your previous experiences and re-examining them using your core motives. For example, an experience where you were hurt because you did not measure up may be an experience that did not align with what motivates you and how you consciously create. Such experiences enable you to understand why you chose what you chose and why you did what you did—and to accept your motive behind it.

Much personal freedom comes when you no longer have to be like someone else who does not have the same motives or ways of conscious creation. You may want to emulate many attributes of these people, but that doesn't mean you need to be just like them or share the same motives and ways of conscious creation.

For example, one common disappointment comes from not being more like our parents. Your parents may feel disappointed that you are not like them, or you may feel sad that you are not like your parents. If you have different motives or ways of conscious creation, you (or they) may feel something is wrong with you. You don't understand why you can't just be more like them.

Again, your results are influenced by motives; your motives and how you consciously create are influenced by your experience. As you read about the different motives, use your exercise results and listen to what feels right. Your conscience can help you choose the best motives and how you consciously create for every situation.

When we are aligned with what motivates us and how we consciously create, what we think and feel causes us to do things that bring us satisfaction. If we do what we think we should do, but not in a way that aligns with our motives or how we consciously create, we won't feel any better after doing it. If you do something that should feel amazing but does not, it likely doesn't align with your core motives.

PLAY 6: YOUR MOTIVES TO CONSCIOUSLY CREATE

Experience   **Progress**

CHOOSE ——— HEART

Think

Visionary   Thinker

Artist   Researcher

Feel

Produce   People

Play   Peace

Do

Manager   Project Manager

Playmaker   Organizer

CONSCIENCE – COURAGE

Before you try to create anything, you need to know *why* and *how* you create. Again, our personality combines our core motive with how we create and what choices we make.

Identify your core motives. Take the number 1 and 2 rankings from each previous section of statements and fill in your motives. Using the key on the next page you can see how these motives correspond to how you consciously create.

For example, if you ranked the statements in the Think section:

a. 2
b. 3
c. 1
d. 4

You would take the answers to this exercise from your number 1 and number 2 choices, (C and A) , look at the key and write in the corresponding words, C. Artist and A. Visionary. These are the two main ways that you consciously create!

Think

1 _____

2 _____

Feel

1 _____

2 _____

Do

1_____

2 _____

KEY:

Think

a. Visionary
b. Thinker
c. Artist
d. Researcher

Feel

a. Produce
b. People
c. Play
d. Peace

Do

a. Manager
b. Project Manager
c. Playmaker
d. Organizer

Remember there is a lot of overlap between your top ways to consciously create. Don't forget about your second place way to create simply because it showed up as second place. Now that you know how you consciously create, you know what to focus on

Join the **www.5Habits.me** community to see what others are experiencing for Play 6.

121

HABIT 3

Be Present
Choose Your Experience Every Day

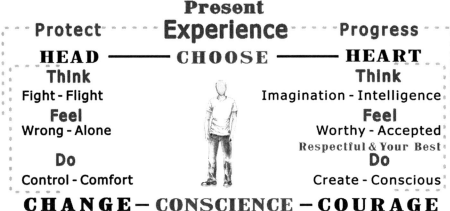

Being Present is experiencing things as they really are.

The dotted paths show us that as we are present to what we are experiencing (protecting in our head and progressing in our heart) we can identify what we are specifically choosing to think, feel and do.

Habit 3 uses the third phase of the head-to-heart framework as shown above.

In habit 3, we will explore what it means to **be present**—to understand our previous experiences and see what is possible to experience. Presence empowers us to choose our experience.

Being present is something I am doing over and over every day. For Christine and me, it is our way of checking in with ourselves to see if we are on course with where we want to go. After some practice, it is usually that simple. When we have tension in our marriage, we are not aligned with each other, so it's up to us to change what we think, feel and do so that we are aligned again.

Yesterday, Christine shared with me an exciting thing that had happened to her. Rather than responding in excitement back, I made a critical observation about what happened. It was very insensitive, even though I had only wanted to help her even more. Christine was crushed.

I walked away thinking: *why is she so sensitive? My intentions are good*! It took me a few minutes to be present to what I was thinking and even to the fact that I was feeling hurt. I looked internally and realized I was able to choose to think and feel something different. Once I stepped back, I could see that I had dampened her excitement. I hadn't even responded to her good news! My comment truly was insensitive.

I apologized and she asked if we could try again so that she could have a new experience with me. Verbatim, she told me her exciting news again and I responded differently this time. I told her how excited I was and I really meant it. We are going through this process of being present in our marriage over and over. We do it over and over because it is the only way we progress. And it gets easier and happens with greater frequency as we put the reps in. It's the process of being courageous—*being you* by *being present*.

CHAPTER 7

Experience Choice
Your Choices Make Up Your Life

"You have brains in your head. You have feet in your shoes. You can steer yourself any direction you choose. You're on your own. And you know what you know. And you are the one who'll decide where to go."

~Dr. Seuss, *Oh, The Places You'll Go!*

I value my ability to choose more than anything else in my life. It is what makes my life mine. My choices make up my life. Without the ability to choose for myself, I am not living my life but living a life decided or determined by someone else.

We all have experiences that affect our choices—*previous experiences* that shape what we think, feel and do or *present experiences* that direct us to think, feel and do something. These experiences affect what we choose, and yet they are not the root cause of what we choose.

I am not controlled by what happens around me. I am a free agent, able to choose for myself and to consciously create. I am not held hostage by my previous or present experiences.

If we can make this separation, we can be free—free to choose for ourselves, regardless of our experiences. To some this may sound unreal or impossible. But we are free to choose, regardless of what we experience, whether we believe it or not.

Obviously our experiences impact what we choose, but ultimately we choose how we think, feel and what we do about our experiences. We may have the same experience as another person, but we experience something completely different. I'm always surprised when this happens. Siblings grow up in the same home with the same rules and parents, but they describe their childhood differently. Have you ever been asked a question when the answer seems apparent, and yet many people see it very differently? This can be as simple as deciding what to call your team or as complex as resolving a dilemma that has two different points of view.

You may be thinking about something in your life, "If I were able to choose, regardless of my previous experience, there is no way I would be choosing this."

Although we have the ability to choose, we have patterns of choosing that put us on autopilot. We choose them, but it's a decision by default because we don't believe there is another choice. These patterns are passed down to us, most often from our family and friends, or we cultivate the pattern with habitual choices. We float along with the culture around us, unaware that another way to do things even exists.

These patterns of choosing become part of us. We become the label "I am".

I am smart. Smart people do _____

I am not smart. People who are not smart do _____

I am nice. Nice people do _____

I am mean. Mean people do _____

I am pretty. Attractive people do _____

I am ugly. Ugly people do _____

I am capable. Capable people do _____

I am incapable. Incapable people do not _____

At first, you may think that you should think kindly about yourself. You are smart and not ignorant, nice not mean, attractive not ugly. That may be true, but you have a pattern of thinking that does not allow you to choose because of who you are (or *think* you are).

I know many people who consider themselves *attractive* who can't choose for themselves regardless of their experiences what they think, feel and do when it comes to their body. They do not allow themselves to be in public unless they are looking as attractive as possible. They base their value on how they look. The money they spend is controlled by what can help them maintain their looks. If they don't measure up, or if someone else is more attractive than they are, they feel inferior, insecure, of no worth. They are ruled by their belief: *I am attractive.*

I know many people who consider themselves *nice* who can't choose for themselves regardless of their experiences what they think, feel and do when it comes to their feelings. They do not allow themselves to think negatively about any situation because nice people don't think things like that. They don't hold others accountable because nice people don't say anything bad about others. They can't be honest about things because they're controlled their belief: *I am nice.*

I know many people who consider themselves unintelligent who can't choose for themselves regardless of their experiences what they think, feel and do when it comes to their mind. They choose not to present their ideas because they worry it will be shut down. They don't solve problems unless told to because unintelligent people don't do that. For the rest of their lives, they make the easier choice because they don't want to break past their hindered intelligence. The job they have, the person they marry—every choice is clouded by their belief: *I am not intelligent.*

Why can't people choose for themselves? Even if they are unintelligent, nice or attractive, they still have unhealthy thoughts and feelings and beliefs about themselves that prevent them from getting what they really want.

Assets can give us great results in the moment, but getting what we really want in life is a choice, not a result from words that describe us.

Again, what we all really want is to feel worthy and accepted. The only way we can feel worthy and accepted is by being respectful and being our best self.

One thought pattern that we all buy into is this: *if I could do _____ I would be happy.*

Satisfaction may happen for a moment, but unless what we do enables us to be who we want to be, it does not last. If we do something that assists us in our progression in who we are being, then it lasts. Satisfaction is never a one-time experience—it is a pattern we develop.

The actions we take, what we do, are a natural result of how we think and feel. How we think and feel comes from who we are being. Who we are being is a result of what we choose. What we choose is a reflection of what we think and feel.

One of the biggest complaints Christine has in our marriage is that I am not accountable for my choices. My pattern is to explain why I made the choice. I explain what I experienced and the logic behind the choice. My choice is then justified and I am not in the wrong. Right?

Wrong. She wants me to be accountable for my choices and their effects. She does not want me to feel bad about my choice and suffer (too much), but she wants me to see the effect it has on her. It is hard for me to be accountable first and not explain why I did what I did because I was not trying to hurt her. Yet without being accountable, I don't acknowledge I had a choice. I can explain my choices extensively, but it's painful to require her to change and adjust to how I do things. Until I acknowledge with accountability that I have a choice, I can't choose otherwise.

As Stephen R. Covey said, "You can choose the action but not the consequences." Ultimately, timeless principles govern.

The pattern of how to choose what we experience, regardless of what experiences happen to us, has never been mapped out. It has been talked about and explained, but the process has been unclear. Along with most people, you would probably agree that you get to choose; and yet, until you experience choosing over and over until it is a habit, it does not seem realistic.

My greatest desire is for you to experience what it is like to choose your experience—to be present to where you are and to choose who you are being. When you are present to who you are being, you can take the next step. You can make the next choice.

If we are not present to where we are, it's tough to take the next step. Ignorance is not bliss. Being present means opening our eyes to what we are choosing and taking accountability for how our choices have given us what we have in life. Our choices have put us where we are. And we have the power to change. It takes tremendous effort and courage to be present, to call it like it is. Life will give us the experiences we need so that we become present.

This often occurs because we are weary from the constant pain of feeling wrong and alone. So we give up trying to do what we think we have to do, what we think others expect of us, what someone like us is supposed to do. We can simply be who we are and where we are. *Being present* means that I'm not harsh to myself, living in constant disappointment with myself, because I'm satisfied with the effort I'm giving and respectful to myself. I can choose my thoughts, emotions and actions. Since I'm not weary anymore, I have the energy to examine what is happening in my mind, in my heart and in my life.

The head-to-heart playbook helps you see your need to create this pattern and experience the pattern—if you choose to experience it. This may be challenging because you may believe you are so smart that you don't need any more information because your life is going well already. But what if there is more—something you never imagined that could take your life to the next level? This may inversely be challenging because you may believe you are so unintelligent that you have no idea how to apply all these new and strange concepts in your life. But what if you tried it a few times and saw a change? What if it was simple to follow a pattern?

Your ability to learn this process will come as you learn to respect yourself and others, be your best, be present and take the next step. All the truths you now have will work with this process. As you expand what is possible and be yourself, this process will become your own. I'm simply showing you the way to examine yourself so that you can get what you want out of your life. When you immerse yourself in this process, it becomes how you choose your experience.

As Socrates said, "An unexamined life is not worth living."

Our ability to choose our experience—no matter what chaos happens around us—is a skill we develop over time. It's the hardest skill we will develop because so many skills change when you exercise your power to choose. The ability to be grateful, forgive, express, accept, love and create—all start with choice. Choice is the origin of what we think, feel and do. It is not the result of what we think, feel and do.

Life Experience

Three of our greatest questions have always been: *1) Why are we here? 2) Where did we come from?* and *3) Where are we going?* These three questions address our lifespan—encompassing our previous, present and possible experience in mortality—and even before and beyond mortality.

Why are we here? What is the purpose of life? Clearly we are born with agency—the freedom to choose our responses to the conditions, circumstances and conditioning of our lives.

We are here to learn how to wisely choose our experience. This will only happen when we have the courage to change what we think, feel and do.

To fully answer the question *why are we here,* we must understand *where am I now, where have I been* and *where am I going.* Once we know the answers to these three questions, we can then choose our experience wisely.

Yes, I realize that some experiences choose you—they just happen. They act on you. You don't get to choose all the stuff that happens to you. You don't get to choose your body type and physical features. You don't get to choose your parents. Human life is set up so that for the first decades of our development, we are vulnerable to those with more power and life experience than us. Sadly, people in positions of power deeply hurt others all the time. That can happen in many different ways without your choice in the matter.

But we do get to choose what we experience—we can choose what we think, feel and do. We can learn and progress from experience, and we can consciously create our experience.

In order to choose our experience, we must understand choice as the ability to freely think, feel and do—regardless of what experience happens to you.

Choice is using our imagination and intelligence to consciously create. Being present affords us many possible choices. When present, we can choose. We have the courage to change what we think, feel and do. Choice is not to have what happens to us decide our experience, but for us to decide what we will experience.

What we experience is not controlled by our experience. *Experience* is what happens to us. *What we experience* is what we choose to think, feel and do about our experience.

We do what we do because of the experiences we have and what we choose to think, feel and do about them. To change that pattern, we must have new experiences—choosing to think, feel and do something different.

This is not a momentary decision, but a process of choosing what we experience over time. This is why it is so difficult to choose what we experience. We tend to allow our previous experience to define who we are. This stops us from asking *who am I* and keeps us from the truth. Blinded, we then believe that the answer to *who am I* is the sum of our previous choices and that these determine what we experience and what is possible for us— now and in the future.

We will never exceed what we believe is possible for us. Feelings of being wrong and alone, unworthy and unaccepted, choke the life right out of us.

In truth, we are not our choices. Rather, our choices are a reflection of what we are choosing to experience. What we experience is the result of our choices.

So, do we have a choice, or do our previous experiences determine what is possible for us? Does our life experience—from birth to adulthood—determine the choices and possibilities available to us? Do the things that happen to us, bad and good, choose for us?

Is it nature or genetic make-up that enables some people to choose while denying others the ability or right to choose? It is not our nature, nurturing or conditioning that determines what we experience—we choose what we experience. This is both the most liberating truth and most painful reality. If we choose what we experience, whatever we are experiencing now is the result of our choices—the pain, the sorrow, the peace and the joy.

Until now you may have believed you had no choice over your thoughts, feelings, choices and experience. You still may believe you have no choice. You can readily think of experiences that are out of your control. True, you cannot choose if some things happen or not. However, you must take accountability for what you experience. True, you can't choose all that happens to you—your choice comes in what you experience.

You are responsible for what you experience. Others are responsible for what they experience. But you are not your experiences. You are not your failures, losses or victories. These experiences assist you in choosing to be you. You are you, and the best way to know who you are is to listen to your conscience: *I am not my experiences; what I choose is up to me.*

Why do we keep choosing some painful things over and over? How can we choose to let those go? Just recognizing what you are experiencing is the first step. You are *present* to your experience, and now you can make another choice. You can choose to keep feeling deficient about not choosing, or you can choose something different. What is something else you could choose?

Why do we choose to feel wrong—why can we not be okay with our choices? If we don't feel bad, we will not change. We have all used *feeling bad* as motivation to change. We've been motivated by these feelings. But has feeling bad ever helped you to change?

You have two basic choices: 1) to feel bad about your choices but not change and 2) to change and not feel bad. We all go back and forth between these two extremes. In reality, you have hundreds of choices, and you will make more than just one choice. You feel bad about many choices so you will need to make a lot of new choices to choose your new experience.

What is another choice you could make? You could pick one choice you have made previously and plan to do it differently. Which choice will you change?

For example, suppose that you keep arguing with your father. You may need to make a dozen new choices in order to change this experience with your dad. Are you ready and willing to make those new choices? You need to recognize when you are not present, meaning not being respectful and being your best self, so you can step back, become present and make a new choice. You need to examine what you are thinking when you argue with your dad. What does it mean that you are having a difference of opinion? What does it mean about you? About him?

Examine those thoughts and open up your mind to the possibility of it meaning something different. As you choose to think something different, you can feel something different and then act differently towards your dad. Your dad might potentially make new choices, but regardless you will have a new experience. He may never say sorry or treat you how you treat him, but what you experience will be what you need. We cannot choose for others to give themselves what they need. We can only choose for ourselves and show them our new choice. So even if he does not follow your lead, you will keep going—because you want to choose for yourself. Because you love him, you can choose to show it regardless of what he chooses. Your experience is not controlled by your father.

Why is it so painful to make a new choice? It is painful for two reasons. First, others may not want us to change. They may not encourage or support us because they feel left behind. Second, we often do not want to change. It is painful to change because our previous choice has been protecting us from feeling something, from having to do something, from taking accountability for what is happening, from feeling wrong and from changing my perception of who *I am*.

I am is the way we see ourselves. Statements that begin with *I Am* are part of us; without them we are not fully ourselves. Whether it is something healthy or unhealthy, we don't know how to be without it. This is why we can't just stop doing something without adding something back in. Actions come from what we think and feel about who we are. If we want to change our actions, we have to examine what we think and feel about who we are.

It can be so painful to change because in order to change we need to examine the thoughts and feelings that lead to our actions. We cannot successfully change our actions while ignoring the feelings and thoughts they are based on. Those feelings and thoughts will not align with the new actions, so our actions will never be sustainable. In order to change, we must fully feel what we feel until it moves us to change. We can't ignore the feelings. We can't pretend we don't feel them. We must clean out the wound in order for it to heal. It is painful, and that pain has a purpose.

PLAY 7: WHO AM I?

This play is to find out who you are—not what you are feeling. Who are you? You are worthy and accepted. When you feel wrong and alone, know that your conscience is instructing you to change—to move from feeling wrong and alone, to feeling worthy and accepted. When you fill in the blanks to the statements *I am* _____ and *I am not* _____, go with your first instinct—don't stop to think. You may be surprised by what comes to mind as you are writing.

Present
Experience

Protect | | Progress

HEAD ——— **CHOOSE** ——— **HEART**

Think | | Think

I AM NOT_____   I AM _____

_____   _____

_____   _____

_____   _____

_____   _____

_____   _____

CHANGE— CONSCIENCE — COURAGE

Join the **www.5Habits.me** community to see what others are experiencing for Play 7.

CHAPTER 8

Experience Conscience
You Face Healthy and Unhealthy Choices

"Labor to keep alive in your breast that little spark of celestial fire called conscience."

~George Washington

How can you know if you are making the right choice? Your conscience shows you what to choose. There is a lot of trial and error, but you can always get back on track. Your conscience can be your guide if you choose. When you betray your conscience, you forget how to follow it. You can learn how to follow the conscience again by becoming present. Ask yourself: *Am I being respectful of others? Am I being my best?* Being present makes it easier to recognize your conscience, and listening to your conscience helps you to remain present. The two go hand in hand to help you live the life you want.

Our ability to choose regardless of our experience determines the quality of our life. The quality of those choices is based on our ability to follow our conscience. Our conscience knows what to choose when our mind does not. When we have experiences, we can learn from them by listening to our conscience. It understands far more than our mind. Our mind helps us learn from our experiences, whereas our conscience helps us understand what we are experiencing—going from what we know to how we feel about it.

Healthy and Unhealthy

We have all heard the aphorism: *let your conscience be your guide*. We usually think in terms of right and wrong, black and white, and that is what our conscience will tell us to do. That is true with how our conscience works, but it only scratches the surface.

Our conscience guides us through our feelings. Our feelings are messengers. The two primary messages the conscience sends us are to change or have courage to continue. When we understand our emotions, we are free to fully experience them. We no longer see emotions as bad and good but as different messages. Certainly some messages are more painful than others, but all messages can help get us where we need to go.

We can feel the exact same emotions in *healthy* and *unhealthy* ways. By *healthy*, I refer to what nourishes us. By *unhealthy*, I refer to what does not. For example, the emotion of *sadness* is often labeled as *unhealthy*, yet that is not always the case. If you were sad because you worked for years to produce a result that did not come to fruition, sadness would be a perfect way for you to express yourself. Thinking that something would happen and not reaching those expectations would naturally and normally cause sadness.

The problem occurs when the feeling of sadness spills over into *who you are*. You repeat the experience over and over. You relive the experience daily even though it happened years ago. You are controlled by the sadness, anger or jealousy. You miss out on new experiences because you can't let go of what you're experiencing. You can't move through the feeling and follow what the feeling is telling you. There are lessons to learn with every experience. Our emotions signal to us what to learn from those experiences. Without the conscience sending these messengers, we would never know to change. We would repeat mistakes.

Ironically our emotions are there so we do not repeat the experience, so we can change and avoid pain. Yet often, because those emotions are so strong, we hold on to them and repeat the experiences in our mind each time as if it happened anew. We are misinterpreting the messages that our conscience is sending us through our emotions! If we can learn to feel the emotion of the experience and listen to our conscience, we can then choose a new experience. This may not be the last time we feel it, but with every experience we will progress. The emotions move us forward, opening our eyes to new ways of thinking and doing.

The end solution is not finding what will take away those feelings. Have you ever heard the big burly father scolding his son to stop crying? *Be a man!* The son can change the action of crying, but his emotions and thoughts are still there, unresolved, only stifled. Our feelings serve a purpose. We need men and women who are willing to feel and listen to what those feelings are telling them. We will never stop feeling these feelings, regardless of how much we progress. These feelings are what make us feel alive. A robot can't feel. How many times have you felt like a robot, just clocking in and out? Robotic lives lack the benefits of being human, feeling the joy and the pain, the ups and the downs and the satisfaction from figuring things out.

The reason we see a sad movie is not to look down on the characters, grateful we don't have pathetic lives. We watch a sad story so we can feel with them. We want to feel emotions that are healthy so that we progress. Emotional progress translates on a scale of looking inward to looking around us. We also shift from feeling the emotions primarily for ourselves and then for others. We feel what they are feeling and feel connected to them. The only way to feel connected is through emotions.

Human connection has morphed so many ways because of technology. Think of the connections we make through cell phones, blogs, e-mail, text, Skype, Facebook, Twitter, Snapchat, Instagram and Pinterest. We use emoticons because words are not enough to fully express how we feel on a screen. So many miscommunications occur because the connection is technological, and the human emotion doesn't penetrate the technology. Healthy, accurate, emotional connection is vital to healthy relationships. Our conscience sends the emotions, and it is up to us to learn how to correctly discern what our emotions mean.

Our bond with others is forged deeply through emotion. Being understood is a powerful human need. We gravitate towards those who can understand us. If we are stuck in our emotions, instead of moving healthily through them, we look for others in the same boat as we are. When we bond in unhealthy ways with others who can understand us, we only focus on the pain of the emotions. When we are bound in healthy ways, we can feel the pain, understand the pain together and yet focus on the possibility beyond the pain. We are not held captive by the pain. The pain is not a watermark on everything we experience for the rest of our lives.

Our conscience conveys to us individually what to do next. We have experiences unique to us that shape our gifts and opportunities. We can all be different and yet be guided by our conscience to find what we need because universal truths guide us all. Universal principles govern us and our conscience informs us of our next step, regardless of what our neighbor is doing. There is no cookie-cutter conscience guide, only universal truths, principles that guide us as we are being present. For example, just like the universal laws of gravity and relativity, the true principle of the Golden Rule is also universal.

There is nothing magical or mythical about your conscience as your guide—no *Jiminy Cricket* is telling you everything you should do. My goal is to show you how to experience conscience for yourself and to help you recognize that promptings are already happening to you. However, until you experience conscience for yourself, my words will not do it justice. Your previous experiences will determine what you choose to do with my words. For now, please keep an open mind to the possibility of, as Stephen R. Covey put it, "educating and obeying your conscience."

If you were to ask yourself, *Have I felt my conscience guide me to stay away from making an unhealthy choice?* And if you were to stop and listen within, I think you would hear the answer, *Yes.*

These emotions are messengers. They influence your thoughts. It is your voice telling you *yes,* which is a result of listening to your conscience. Your emotional pain is a direct result of not following your conscience. Your emotional peace is a direct result of following your conscience. The question is this: *are you willing to follow your conscience?*

As we move forward, you will start to understand and experience following your conscience. Where you are now is the perfect place to start. The goal is progress, not perfection.

In order to wisely and consistently choose our experience, we must listen to our conscience. When we don't follow our conscience regarding what we think, feel and do, we will sense it by our head or heart. Just as our bodies have many ways to tell us whether something is healthy or unhealthy, so does our conscience.

The primary way the body does this is by how we feel, and the primary way the conscience does this is also by how we feel. If we overeat, we feel sick. If we don't eat at all, we feel weak. When we feed ourselves lies, we feel sick. If we don't feed ourselves the truth about who we are, we feel weak. We may then make choices based on thoughts that are not true.

Both our bodies and our conscience tell us to change based on how we feel. When we have an experience, we tend to think, feel and do what we have previously done. Unless we're conscious of that pattern and know why we are choosing it, we can't create anything new or different.

The hardest part of this process is changing what we believe our feelings are telling us. We have been trained to believe there are good feelings like joy and peace . . . and bad feelings like anger and sadness. We have been trained to not feel angry or sad; if we do, something must be wrong with us, since no one else is feeling that way—hence, we feel that we are alone.

We can look at our feelings as messengers, telling us to change or have the courage to continue. Our conscience sends us messages based on our choices. We can only make sense of these messages when we recognize what thought caused the feeling.

Feeling Wrong and Alone

For example, if we feel embarrassed we may think *I should never do this again.* Before the feeling, came the conscious or unconscious thought *Everyone hates me*. The feeling comes from this thought. When you think *Everyone hates me*, *Something is wrong with me* or *I am alone* your conscience is telling you with your feelings that this thought is not healthy and to leave the thought alone.

When you think *Everyone hates me* and you feel embarrassed, wrong and alone and you never again want to do what made you embarrassed, your conscience is trying to tell you that something is wrong. So often we interpret the feeling of embarrassment as *something is wrong with me*. What is wrong is the thought. Your feeling of embarrassment is actually telling you that your thought is wrong.

Examine the thought: everyone hates me. Does everyone hate me? Is there anyone on the planet who doesn't hate me? Why don't they hate me? Did I choose something that I might never want to choose again? Sure. But should I be hated for one choice? No. I'm trying my best and I can try again and I can change to try something different. It doesn't mean that everyone hates me. Some people might truly hate me. But hatred could be the best strategy they learned in playing the game. We can find peace knowing that everyone is trying their best. Malicious intent is rare but happens. How someone treats you is an accurate mirror to how they feel about themselves. Unexpressed feelings could be the main culprit. We boil over onto each other when we don't properly expel our emotions. I probably brought up a feeling for them that was a previous experience. They are allowed to hate me. But I don't have to be controlled by their hatred.

> **What is an experience where you have misunderstood your thoughts?**
>
> *Christine: I was talking to my mom and she paused for a long time and I thought she was disappointed in me with what I shared with her. I asked her and she said she was just thinking of how what I said applied to her.*

The *5 Habits to Lead from Your Heart* principles are not dependent on everyone around you realizing their mistakes and changing. They are independent of the choices and actions of others. Your success and happiness is based only on your willingness to educate and obey your own conscience.

Everyone around you can be running the "wrong and alone" play, over and over, never stepping outside of themselves. But you have the freedom to listen and to choose, no matter what is going on around you. No one is going to make it easy for you. People are running plays that don't work for them and their pain may affect you. But your conscience gives you the messages you need so that you can choose.

When we have an experience and have thoughts that align with our conscience, we feel worthy and accepted. We're not worried what others think of us. We know we are of worth. We feel at peace and accept where we are presently. Our conscience tells us to have courage to keep doing what we are doing. What we think, feel and do is exactly what we should think, feel and do. The challenge is understanding our conscience since we all have different experiences. Hence, our version of *being respectful* and *being our best* is different. Our consciences are different.

We are only able to listen to our conscience where we are presently. Our conscience only brings up a few things to change and a few things to have courage to continue. It does this so that we are not overwhelmed. Without this filtering we are overcome with feelings of being wrong and alone over a lifetime of choices. We would be conscious of hundreds of things we should create all at once. If we ask ourselves a question and listen to our conscience, we will know what to do. Our conscience lights up the next few steps as we clear the darkness before us.

Wrong Can Feel So Right

Feeling wrong and alone is often the root cause of lose/lose or win/lose in our relationships. Whether you consider yourself the winner or the loser, it's a relationship set up to fail. In fight-or-flight mode, feeling attacked, we line ourselves up against an enemy. We make enemies all around us. We gain our value, our worth and acceptance, on being right and someone else has to be wrong. Or we are wrong and alone against those who think they are right. This is considered normal and acceptable behavior in most cultures. But the abundant choice is to accept our own personal effort and the effort of others. When we feel wrong and alone or feel threatened that someone is trying to make us wrong and alone, we can courageously examine what we are feeling, identifying if we are following the ground rules or not. Are we allowing others to follow the ground rules? Are we going for a real win or trying to win at someone else's expense?

Examining our feelings keeps us from going around in circles of wrong and alone. Ignore any possibility that keeps you from feeling worthy and accepted. When you feel wrong and alone, you may tell yourself or others: *you always act this way. You should be ashamed of yourself. I blame you. It's your fault. You never help around the house. I'm the victim here! You make me so mad! You never see it my way. I'm always the one that has to do this.*

When we feel wrong and alone, we pit ourselves against others and gather evidence that makes us justified in the position. We look for ways to feel right. We use shame and blame to deflect responsibility for actions. We love to use *always* and *never* statements so that there is no possibility for reconciliation or change. It feels good to stay in the wrong because it's not our fault. Anyone in our situation would be on our side, since the offense seems so blatantly wrong. There is no accountability or possibility in being alone. Wrong feels so right.

How could you stop blaming others?

Christine: I could stop blaming others by feeling right in healthy ways instead of needing to feel right in all my relationships.

Worthy and Accepted

Although our consciences differ, at the core, they tell us the same basic thing: *I am worthy.* I am valuable regardless of my previous experience.

When we have experiences that cause us to feel we are wrong and alone, we feel unhealthy. Our conscience tells us to change. When we have experiences that cause us to feel worthy and accepted, we feel healthy. Our conscience is telling us to have courage to continue, no matter what others think of us. Feeling a range of emotions is healthy and normal. It means our conscience is sending us messages. The problem is . . . we don't understand the messages.

The emotions we feel are labeled as *wrong*, and therefore, *something must be wrong with me for feeling them. I feel alone and believe no one else feels this way.*

Wrong = Feeling disconnected from ourselves

Alone = Feeling disconnected from others

These thoughts and feelings become an unhealthy cycle of sickness. If we don't understand what our conscience is telling us, what we experience is that *something is wrong with me, I am alone* and *no one else feels this way.* When we listen to and obey our conscience, we are healed. We just have to feed our conscience the truth and then follow it.

When we look at newborn babies, we see that they are of worth and accept them as they are, even though they have not done anything yet. It is difficult, however, to see ourselves this way. As we become older and have experiences, we stop believing we are of inherent worth and we don't accept where we are presently. The only difference between us and a baby is we have experiences where we do not follow our conscience. We then believe *something is wrong with me. I am alone. I am worthless. I am not worthy of success.* In reality, our conscience is telling us to choose to change or choose to have the courage to continue.

We are either fundamentally worthy and accepted or fundamentally wrong and alone. If something is wrong with us and we are alone, life is meaningless pain. If we are worthy and accepted, life is a chance to learn to choose to experience the truth of who we are.

Understanding Feelings

Our conscience lights the way for us with our feelings. When we misunderstand our conscience and feel wrong and alone, we feel dark and cold. A lack of light is darkness. A lack of warmth is cold. A lack of following our conscience is emotional pain. We are not the cold, darkness and emotional pain, but we feel them when we do not choose the warmth and light of our conscience. The emotional pain only exists because we choose it. It has a purpose, if you let it lead you to change.

We need to understand what is going on when a feeling comes. There are many words to describe our emotions, and usually each emotion has an opposite: happy or sad, angry or pleased, disappointed or fulfilled, hopeful or depressed, calm or anxious, excited or bored, dissatisfied or content, embarrassed or proud, brave or afraid.

Feelings are not good and bad emotions. Every emotion serves a purpose to communicate feedback based on what is going on. So, feel your emotions. Imagine a mailbox full of unopened letters addressed to you from your conscience. They are stacking up and you aren't even willing to touch them. You are missing out on instructions and directions that would be very helpful as you are making important life decisions and building valuable relationships. Feelings that aren't felt are like sealed envelopes, and one match could ignite the entire pile.

Once you feel your feelings, examine what your conscience is telling you with your feelings. The feeling has a purpose. What is the purpose of this feeling? Open the letter from your conscience and find out what it means. If you are feeling sad, you either need to make a change or have the courage to continue what you are doing. Each emotion brings you to that crossroad. When you choose to feel and to make sense of your emotions, you can figure out what to do with your feelings.

PLAY 8: WORTHY AND ACCEPTED

We are *worthy and accepted*, but we often play from *wrong and alone*. In our relationships we often easily accept the worth of others without really believing our own worth. We think that others have value, but if anyone knew how much we struggled or how inconsistent our results were, they would see we are worthless. So we think we have a lot to hide. We avoid authentic connections with others.

Do you feel worthy and accepted, regardless of your previous experience? Do you ever feel that you have to prove your value? Are you acting out of fear instead of freedom? Are you harder on yourself than you are on anyone around you? Do you have many friends and Facebook "likes", plenty of Pins and Snapchats, and yet no one is there when you really need a friend? All of the results in your life show how socially connected you are, but you are feeling wrong and alone.

We need to believe that we are worthy and accepted and make choices to act based on that accurate assessment of ourselves—we are enough, regardless of previous experience. We don't base our value on whether or not others find value in us. We don't compare ourselves based on our results because we aren't feeling wrong and alone or trying to make others wrong and alone. When we feel our worth and accept ourselves, we have these thoughts: *I really tried my best. I am enough. Good for you. You deserve that. Well, that didn't happen the way I imagined. Let me try again. I'm so happy for you. This is important to me, so I'll figure it out.*

We do not look at ourselves as deficient or defunct. Our best effort is sufficient. We can move forward. We can accept the value of ourselves and others. Our conscience communicates our worth and acceptance when it sends us feelings of peace, satisfaction, love, contentment. These feelings help us accept our worth.

Think of an experience where you have felt worthy and accepted and relive it. Write out on the diagram what you were thinking, feeling and doing.

Present
Experience
CHOOSE ———— **HEART**

Progress

Think

_____

_____

Feel

_____

_____

Do

_____

CONSCIENCE – COURAGE

Join the *www.5Habits.me* community to see what others are experiencing for Play 8.

CHAPTER 9

Experience Change
Gain Happens When Pain Mandates

Tale as old as time, True as it can be
Barely even friends, then somebody bends, unexpectedly
Bittersweet and strange, finding you can change
Learning you were wrong.
~Disney's Beauty and the Beast

Perhaps we can best learn to experience change vicariously by revisiting another dialogue between Christine and myself.

"Why do you act like a hurt puppy when we disagree?"

"Why are you surprised that I do this when you yell at me?"

"I am just telling you how I feel. Stop taking it so personally."

"We are married! How could it not be personal?"

"If you were not so sensitive, we could figure this out."

"If you weren't so abrasive, I would want to work it out."

"Alright. This obviously isn't working . . ."

"Let's talk about this when we can have a heart-to-heart."

"OK. Let's talk again after we have both worked through what we are experiencing."

After we let some time pass ...

"Can we talk? I am ready to answer your question of why I am sensitive. I realized that I go into protection mode with my flight response. When you yell I feel like it's because you think something is wrong with me. I can totally see how I'm in my head when I withdraw. I'm trying to protect myself. I'm sorry for not being in my heart over this."

"Well, I know why I am so harsh. We are complete opposites. I protect myself by fighting. I would never hit you, but I definitely try to bully you to get what I want when I yell. And I usually do get what I want because you cower to me. But I don't want to fight you. I don't want to be that kind of spouse. When you withdraw, I feel alone and I'm freaking out trying to get control or I can't protect myself. I am sorry for yelling."

"I am sorry for reacting. I don't want to withdraw from you and leave you alone by withdrawing."

"I love you."

"I love you, too, babe. What is a possibility for next time?"

The 5 Habits have been so impactful on our marriage. We have this common language and understanding to be able to quickly get to the roots of our many problems. Our language is so inundated with the vocabulary of habits of the heart because each word means exactly what we are going through: protect, flight, wrong, control, head. Defining your experience lends so much hope. It has helped us avoid unnecessary hurt feelings. We simply do not engage head-to-head. It is too detrimental. And if we do, it is only for a few minutes until one of us is reminded that we can't progress when we are trying to protect ourselves. That's not to say we don't get angry because we really do. We just don't lash out at each other while we are angry. We do the work individually so that we can come back, ready to progress together. The head-to-heart framework provides understanding for what is really going on. It helps us to be respectful, be accountable and create as a team from our hearts.

Fight or Flight?

I use the words *head* and *heart* to talk about different parts of our brain. The part of our brain that tells us we need to *change* is our *head*.

Change = To *think, feel and do* differently than we previously have done

Head = Using your *fight/flight* response (lower-back brainstem and cerebellum)

Fight = To protect by force

Flight = To protect by avoiding

When we experience something, we form a thought and feeling about what is happening and often misinterpret the feeling our conscience is sending us. We think we are wrong and alone or that someone else thinks we are wrong, and we prepare to defend ourselves, our *fight* mode, or avoid the person or situation, our *flight* mode.

Fight: the fight play is meant to protect us. We do whatever it takes to protect our position and defend our decision. We try to assert our position through power and not yielding.

Consider this scenario: Your teenager forgot to load the dishwasher after dinner.

You ask, "Can you go back and finish the job, please?"

"No, I didn't forget. In fact, I was just about to do it before you got on my case about it."

"Well, it's usually running by now. I just thought I would remind you."

"I would have plenty of time to do it if I weren't always thinking of you looking over my shoulder, waiting for me to mess up!"

"I didn't mean to make you feel that way."

"Don't worry—you're very good at it. You can do it without even trying. You don't care about me. You're just using me to keep your house clean. There are laws against child labor!"

Fight can play out in many ways, but the most common is pulling the other person into the wrong and alone arena so you can duke it out. We list things to make the other person wrong so we can be right and win. Bullying your way into a win works until you meet a bully bigger than you. Some people fight for years before they learn there is a different choice. Fighting is incredibly effective if you are in a position of power. And it's incredibly addicting if you're surrounded by people who cower to your demands. Fight is also effective because it establishes credibility and reputation. When others are afraid of you, you don't even have to waste time fighting them.

Flight: we may choose to protect ourselves by fleeing. We avoid confrontation and connection because that might convert into pain. We try to safeguard our position through retreat. No matter the cost, we will not bear arms.

Consider this scenario: Your teenager did not finish his chores.

You ask, "Can we talk about the chores you never finished Saturday?"

"Fine, I'm just an idiot! I don't deserve this family."

"That's not what I'm saying."

"No really, I'll just go. I'm not even going to try to explain anything to you."

"I'd really like to know what's going on with you."

"No. I'll be in my room when you're done lecturing me."

Flight can play out in many ways, but the most common way is avoiding connection so there is no resolution. We cower, whimper and surrender without trying to work through anything. Protecting by *Flight* is incredibly effective because you control your experience through avoidance and you stay away from hard things. You put an incredible amount of energy into avoiding, but you are not required to expend any energy into figuring out your problems.

The fight/flight response is useful when we are in danger; however, it can be damaging when we use our head to choose when there is no danger. That part of the brain is telling us to change, but we think it is telling us to survive an attack—fight or flight.

Control or Comfort?

When we are in our heads and have thoughts of fight or flight, we are usually seeking to gain control or comfort.

Control: even when we gain control over ourselves, others or the situation, we rarely get what we truly want. Control only lets us momentarily escape the feeling of being wrong or alone.

For example, food that is unhealthy for you may taste good and give you energy in the moment, but it will not help you have energy and health long term. This is why we overeat. We can control how we feel for a moment.

Why does control keep us in our head, keep us reacting by fighting and keep us from changing? It silences our inner *raptor* while it is eating. But the raptor will become hungry again within a few hours and must be fed again. In this way, the raptor controls us. The raptor is all about protecting by fight/flight using our head.

An adrenaline rush comes from being in our head because of the risk we take or the danger we feel. This could be the risk of getting hurt or hurting others to get what we want. We get addicted to the rush. The chemicals released by our brain help us to survive. Many experiences—such as when we confront a problem, engage in a conflict or compete for a win—can flood our bodies with the chemicals necessary to protect us from danger. What we think about these situations leads to that feeling. Unfortunately, this rush tells our body the only way to feel alive is to be in danger. So, we put ourselves into danger in order to feel. Yet the danger is not as real as we feel it is, and we become exhausted.

We may feel alive when we are in control. Again, *control* means manipulating our experience for a temporary relief from pain. To stop feeling wrong and alone, we seek control. It's hard to see the forest for the trees when you are in control. One way to identify it is to look for examples in other people's lives where you think they are out of control.

Think: where do I see others as out of control? Well, I see people who are overweight, people who have children that don't obey, people who have too much credit card debt, people who let themselves go after they have children. If someone is out of control in a category, think about yourself in that category. Are you trying to control in the same category? Are you pushing the way you like things done on other people?

Another way to identify if you are running this play is to examine some of your previous feelings. Think of feeling furious. When have you felt furious? Was it when someone tried to take away control of something from you? It could have been somewhere you are exercising control because you are trying to avoid feeling wrong. Were you furious because someone was threatening your experience?

Control is unhealthy because you are manipulating an experience to avoid pain. Control also can mean taking away the right to choose from yourself or from someone else. That is the height of disrespect: your choice taking away someone else's right to choose. Control is also unhealthy because it provides a false sense of connection that won't last.

The healthy way to move out of control is to be present to what you are experiencing and accountable for what you have created. The control play thrives on protecting ourselves from feeling wrong and alone. Control takes away the power to choose. That power can be restored as we move from control back to being present, courageously examining if we are being disrespectful by manipulating our experience.

Where do you seek control?

Christine: I see my children as a reflection of me and I try to control their expressions of themselves so I look good.

Comfort: we may also seek to protect ourselves from being hurt by seeking comfort. We feel alone—and we make sure we are alone. We do not share what we are feeling for fear of being judged. We do not want to connect with others for fear of being hurt. In seeking comfort, we might reject others before they can reject us. Everything we think, feel and do is to avoid pain. But the pain of being alone does not make up for not letting others in. What we do seems to provide us comfort. Comfort is avoiding our experience for a temporary relief from pain. But does it really? Is it really comfortable to be disconnected from others?

This play is so common that it is considered normal; however, this play means ignoring the message from your conscience that something needs to change, taking flight and choosing comfort to avoid being present to our experience. We are not trying our best when we seek comfort. We are avoiding the fight, dodging life so we don't have to live it. We see this play everywhere we look: riding the subway and no one is looking at each other—earphones are in, heads are down, breaking up from a relationship—by text, drowning your sorrows with any substance—food, alcohol, drugs, avoiding human connection, never going for something because you're scared you won't get it and staying where you are because you're scared you can't do any better.

Comfort means that you are engaging in whatever you can to sidestep the pain of being present to what is really going on. Comfort is running away to dodge the pain of being present to what is really going on. Comfort is ultimate avoidance. Engage in the easiest thing that will take all of our attention so we don't have to feel the pain of the fact that we need to change. It's a comfortable place to be. And we go stagnant, accepting the place we are stuck in because to move means pain. Confrontation is not comfortable so you avoid it at all costs because you might be wrong and alone. Accountability is not comfortable so you aren't because you can't risk being wrong and alone. Courage is not comfortable. It seems so far out of your reach, you can't move. You are literally stuck. Progress is not comfortable. It is a mortal enemy to comfort.

Now, you may think that it is good to be in control and comfortable. You are right. The process of going from your head to your heart is one where you go from being in control and comfortable to out of control and uncomfortable. You willingly go through the pain because you know the pain serves a purpose to move you forward and open up more choices for you.

Where are you seeking comfort in your life?

Christine: I seek comfort in food. I will reward myself with something to eat or drink if I'm going through something hard.

One big reason we don't change is because others can be threatened by our change. People don't want to be left behind. Especially in close relationships, we want to feel comfortable. Progress can be threatening to some if they are not used to having their efforts be accepted. It goes back to following the ground rules. Be respectful to yourself and others. Accept your own best effort and the effort of others. Be present to what is really going on. It isn't a stretch at all to think of this as someone's possible response to your change. People in our relationships could be in their head when you make a change. They feel alone and feel something is wrong with them if we change and they don't. They feel left behind. So they will do things to stop you from changing.

When we change, we give others the possibility and permission to change. Change will only happen when it is too painful to continue to be in our head because it no longer gives us comfort and control. Change happens either because our previous way of doing things is painful or we see a new possibility which causes our previous way of doing things to be painful.

We change by having the courage to consciously create leading from our heart. Progress is challenging. What was originally an experience of being in our heart eventually becomes an experience of being in our head. What we consciously created no longer gives us the same level of comfort and control. Our new way of doing things becomes a previous way of doing things.

We can then become present to what we are experiencing and choose a new possible experience. Learning this process is how we progress. It is a conscious creation process of learning to choose our experience. The beauty of this process is that we keep changing, growing and progressing—not because something is wrong with us or because we are alone or because we are unworthy and unaccepted—we change because we are worth it! We change because we accept our present experience and choose to exercise our power to choose—to act, not just to be acted upon or to react. We are like a *lion* rebelling against our head, our desire for comfort and control, leading from our heart, using our imagination and intelligence, to consciously create what we experience. It takes lion-like strength to break free from the way we are used to doing things. The lion is the perfect metaphor for change because of the strength required to courageously choose something different, despite powerful influences around us.

We change because we understand and respond to what our conscience is telling us to do. When Stephen R. Covey was asked, "Of all of the advice you have given people to help them succeed in their private and professional lives, what advice has made the most impact?" He replied, "Educate and obey their conscience." I believe he said this in part because an educated conscience enables us to choose to consciously create change.

Because of what you are experiencing now, you may be ready to change. When you are ready to change, you can go in a moment from using your head to think, feel and do to leading from your heart to think, feel and do. When you are in a circumstance that is so painful that you recognize that you must change and that you have a choice to change to create something new and have the courage to do it—it can happen in an instant.

This head-to-heart framework enables you to consciously and authentically create. This is the process of restoration—to bring back to the original condition. Restoration happens when we stop feeding poison to the raptor, the fight or flight responder, and start feeding truth to the lion, our courageous selves willing to choose our experience.

Story: The Boss Experience

It's Friday, 4 p.m., and I'm hoping that my boss has forgotten about my weekly report due on his desk. It has been a busy week, and the last thing I want to think about is filling out that report.

But here he comes. "Ready for the weekend?" he asks.

"I can't wait." I become more uncomfortable as he keeps standing near me and I keep thinking about my past-due report. Why does he keep chit-chatting? What kind of game is he playing?

He tells me to have a good weekend and leaves. What is he trying to hide? What is he up to?

Although he did not bring up the report, I feel at risk. Should I have said something? Is he testing me? Is he just playing with my emotions and making me feel bad? I don't know if I should talk to him or not. I'm not sure if I'm in hot water or if he doesn't even care about the report. Not knowing is killing me. I don't want to feel like this all weekend. What should I do?

I keep replaying the scenario to look for clues of the boss setting me up. Each time I think about screwing this up, I feel sick. I was supposed to have my report completed and turned in by now. So why was he so nice when he came in? He should have criticized me. When I replay the scene in my mind I can see how he might have been just checking to see how I was. This is driving me crazy! I have agonized over this for 30 minutes. I'm getting nothing done. By now I could have completed the report and turned it in. I am an idiot! I feel terrible. What should I do?

I have decided to get this over with. I need to face the fact that my feelings are not aligned with reality. My boss has never yelled at me or even been sarcastic. Why am I so afraid of him? It's like he is a raptor in my head. If I don't have everything perfectly ready, I feel like he will attack me. It has never happened, but I have had enough bosses to know that it might. I feel that I need to protect myself since every boss will eventually attack me. That's what bosses do.

I can't stand it anymore. I have to do the report and talk to him.

I'm finished and he's walking out of his office.

"Here is this week's report."

"Great. Just put it on my desk, and I will look at it Monday." He puts a ball cap on his head and explains, "I've got to get to my kid's game."

I watch him walk away and realize that it was all in my head. I was freaking out over nothing. He wasn't worried about it. My job's not in danger. He knows I will do it. I always do.

I sink back into my chair and I realize that my fight/flight reaction is a pattern for me. I make things into a big deal and feel horrible.

I decide now to question what I am thinking next time. Is it true? Is that really how it happened? I will no longer allow my previous experience to choose for me. I will no longer let other people control me. I will no longer stay in my comfort zone by withdrawing.

I will respect myself for what I do and not focus on what I can't do or won't do. I will do the same for others. I will do my best, knowing that it is enough. Recognizing my worth and accepting myself will make my work experience so much more productive and enjoyable.

I walk out the office and I feel great about what I choose to change. I am excited to see what I will create next week. This is a feeling I have not had in a long time. I feel complete. I'm completely ready for whatever happens next. I'm completely present to what is happening now.

I'm completely free from anything that held me back previously.

PLAY 9: YIELDING

Try yielding your control by saying *I don't know*. When you yield to the possibility that you have no idea what to do next and yield control and become present, you can admit that you were trying to force what you wanted—and you can then try something different. Yielding with *I don't know* is a powerful play because it is a shortcut. One simple statement moves you automatically from trying to control a situation from your head to being open to possibilities with your imagination, from your heart. There are possibilities you didn't realize existed and you have access to them when you yield.

Write out your response: One experience where I can let go of control and say *I don't know* is...

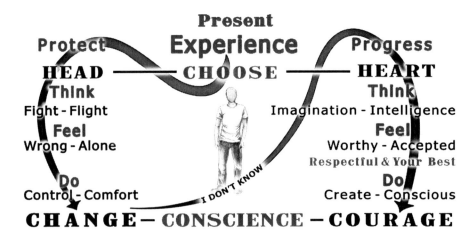

Join the ***www.5Habits.me*** community to see what others are experiencing for Play 9.

HABIT 4

Be Restored

Go from Previous and Present to What's Possible

Previous	Present	Possible
Protect	**Experience**	Progress
HEAD ——	**CHOOSE** ——	**HEART**
Think		**Think**
Fight - Flight		Imagination - Intelligence
Feel		**Feel**
Wrong - Alone		Worthy - Accepted
		Respectful & Your Best
Do		**Do**
Control - Comfort		Create - Conscious

CHANGE — CONSCIENCE — COURAGE

Being Restored is the process of going from our head to our heart using our conscience with previous experience.

The dotted path from previous to present and from present to possible represents being restored. Becoming present to previous experiences allows an opening for a new possible experience. We can then choose to restore that previous experience with this new way to think, feel and do. This is the path of restoration.

Habit 4 uses the fourth phase of the head-to-heart framework as shown above.

We often talk of change in terms of growth, improvement, transition and even transformation. This habit takes another step—toward *restoration*—to be restored to the real, authentic you.

As a young man I wanted nothing more than to find my true love and start a family. I had found the girl I wanted to marry and she wanted to marry me. Last thing for me to do was to meet her parents. She still wanted to take some time to feel like it was the right thing to do because that is what she needed before committing to be my wife.

A short while after I met her parents, she did not feel right about the marriage plans we had made. She broke up with me. I was devastated. I had been broken up with before, but this was different. I had believed on a deep spiritual level that she was the one and I could not see why she did not feel the same way.

I went into a deep depression. It brought up all of the worst thoughts I have ever had about myself. Something was wrong with me. Even a girl that is my perfect match knows something is wrong with me. To you it may not seem like that big of deal, but for me my greatest fear had been realized. I was just not husband material.

I saw her at a party with her new boyfriend and became physically ill. I went home and I was as mad and sad as I had ever been. *Why is this happening to me? What is wrong with me?* After going that low I felt there was nowhere to go but up. I started to question the lies I was telling myself. I started to do the things I used to do: hang out, ask girls out, etc.

In a few months, I had restored how I felt about myself by seeing myself as worthy and accepted. Less than a month after that, I asked out a girl that helped it all make sense. The first thought I had after she walked away was *I could marry her* and four months later, I did.

Four months is crazy fast, but I knew why it did not work the first time. I could clearly see why it would not have been the best for us both. One experience of pain and rejection led me to the other of realizing my greatest hopes and dreams. Yet unless I was willing to go through the restoration process, I would have missed my opportunity to marry Christine. She had just gone through a similar restoration process which is why we were such a great match.

We are not matched well because we are the same, but because we were both willing to be present and restore anything which did not align with where we were headed. We have refined the process over the years, which is why you are able to read this book.

CHAPTER 10

Previous Experience
Ask Yourself, "What Is It Telling Me?"

"Every qualification for success is acquired through habit. People form habits, and habits form futures. If you do not deliberately form good habits, then unconsciously you will form bad ones."

~Albert Gray

Many previous experiences are replicated in the present, and so we have to reflect on and redress the previous experience in order to get the poison out and gain perspective.

When we reflect on previous experiences, we might ask *What was really happening? What was that experience telling me?* We often feel pain when we bring up our previous experiences because we were not being respectful or being our best. This is because we were not present to what our conscience was telling us. To change our experience we need to re-experience the past and then use our heart to heal.

Feel It or Conceal It?

When we have an experience where we are in our head, we can either feel it or conceal it. When we feel it, that feeling enables us to change. When we conceal it, that feeling disables us. We become comfortable with current conditions, and the raptor starts to control us, even paralyze us. We no longer are motivated by the pain to change because we eventually see such pain as normal. We are only open to change when the pain increases again to the point that we can't ignore it.

When we are newborn, everything in life is stimulating. Our senses are keenly alive with sight, touch, smell, taste and sound. Since our brain and body have not experienced these things before, we are alert to every new sensation. Over time, however, we become accustomed to these experiences so we are able to function without suffering from over-stimulation.

If we tell ourselves something poisonous over and over, eventually we numb ourselves to not feel the effects. We are no longer hurt by the poison because we numb ourselves to not experience it fully. In fact, we eventually consider the poison to be *how things are, who we are, who others are* or *what we deserve.*

Even though you do not think the pain or poison is acceptable for others to experience, it becomes our normal because it must become normal for us to survive physically, to succeed socially, to thrive financially or to cope emotionally.

The only way to change is to feel what we are feeling—the fight, the flight, the fright, the frustration, the futility or the failure—to fully experience it and expel it: the anger, the sadness. These painful feelings are telling us to change. So feel it and then change by choosing to consciously create a new experience with your intelligence—your ability to understand experience, to see things as they really are. Consciously use your intelligence to know what has previously worked. Consciously use your imagination to create new possibilities.

What feelings do you need to feel that you are holding back?

Christine: I need to feel angry about something that happened to me in college. I never really got mad about the injustice of it. I just worked through it and moved on. I need to feel mad.

Both Head and Heart

We do not want to ignore our head and go quickly to our heart. Rather we want to completely experience what our head is telling us. We cannot create lasting change unless we truly feel what our conscience is telling us. To remove poisonous thoughts, we have to feel the feelings connected to them. We are then open to choosing to think and feel something new.

Most of us use both head and heart when making decisions. Early in life, we tend to be *all heart*, very impulsive in making decisions. As we age, however, we tend to use more logical, rational and objective reasoning. At times, we ignore our heart and get stuck in our head. Whether we use head or heart may depend on the situation. Developing the ability to use both head and heart adds to our mental and social power.

When I am primarily operating in my head, I tend to be fear-driven. I evaluate everything, perhaps even over-analyze it, and then do nothing (or next to nothing) due to fear and limiting beliefs. This leads to indecision and procrastination. When I invite my heart into the decision making, I can't deny myself the knowledge that *this is the right path for me*. My conscience tells me *this is the way to go*. I don't have all the answers, but I have confidence that I will be guided along the way. Instead of thinking *I should* I think *I could*. And the I *have to* notion is replaced with *I want to*.

After we completely feel with our head, we are open to completely feel with our heart. The courage to experience our head gives us the courage to experience our heart. We can then expel the poison completely without residual effects on our possible experience.

Again, when we eat food that has gone bad, our body knows something is wrong and to vomit out the food. If our body cannot keep the food in because it is too vile, it will force the poison out with a quick exit strategy. It hurts for a moment, but we feel better later.

When we have been poisoned, our conscience is giving us a feeling to leave it alone and that something is wrong with that thought and we need to get it out.

To release the poison, we must fully feel and experience the thought. Until the poison is out, we find it challenging to choose to do anything differently. It would be like trying to eat a healthy meal to counter food poisoning. The only way to counter food poisoning is to get it out of our system, not simply add more food. After the poison is out, you can either learn what not to do next time or you can repeat the same mistake again without any change.

There is a window of time to choose to do something different. After we recover and are back to our normal experience we lose our desire to change. We forget any pain we were in because the crisis has passed. The time between completely feeling what we are feeling and feeling better is the time to choose something different. It is in that moment after we feel sad and fully express it that we can feel hope. It is that moment after we feel angry and let it out that we feel a release and finally feel some peace. If we hold our emotions in, it's like trying to not vomit. We feel horrible and know we will feel better after vomiting, but we also know how painful it will be. So we try to control ourselves by holding it in.

Where do you need to let go?

Christine: I need to let go of trying to please everyone around me. It's killing me.

Gain from the Pain

We experience the same process emotionally. There are healthy and unhealthy ways to express our emotions. The unhealthy way is to vomit emotionally on yourself and others by saying or doing something that we later regret.

There are many plays for expressing our emotions in healthy ways so we don't hurt ourselves or others in the process. This may involve an emotional detox, but we are choosing to do it in a healthy way. You can do this through exercise, talking to someone, writing in a journal, listening to music or anything that lets you feel what you are feeling while letting it out. Don't hold back on this. And recognize what you are doing as it is happening. Being in your head is not bad. It is the catalyst necessary for change. Don't cut yourself short from feeling what your conscience is telling you.

As you experience the moment where the poison is out, that is when you have the courage to change by conscious creation. You will use your intelligence to make a plan. You will use your imagination to see a new solution. You accept yourself where you are at and feel worthy of something more. You consciously create something that will stop the pattern.

The challenge is we are only open to change after we see the problem and experience it. We have to go from our head to our heart to experience the pain and to change.

There are various levels of pain and change—not all of them are severe or dramatic, but all levels follow the same pattern. The key to change is to recognize when you have expelled the poison, whether in a healthy or unhealthy way, and use your heart to consciously create a new experience. Our head releases the poison but it will just come back stronger. If we use our head to release the poison and our heart to heal, we can consciously create a new experience.

I know someone who was so annoyed by how people chewed. She would just get frustrated and worked up and angry about people chewing near her. And now, 20 years later, she's okay with being near people who chew their food differently from her. She's not mad about it. Sometimes it's easy and quick and other times it's a longer process. But when you know the pattern, you will trust the process, no matter the complexity of your pain.

EXAMPLE: FROM PREVIOUS TO PRESENT

The Boss Experience continued…

My experience with my last boss was that I would come to work afraid for my job every day. The company was down-sizing during the economic recession, and people were being let go. No manager ever talked to us. So, I tried to avoid conversation and eye contact. Finally, all of us lost our jobs when the doors closed after a year of living paranoid.

I was only thinking about survival and feeding my family. I thought if I could avoid the boss, I could avoid getting fired. I only thought of not making mistakes to give anyone a reason to let me go. I thought I would lose my house if I didn't have this job. I would never get a new job, even after 15 years in the industry. I thought I wasn't relevant to another company. I thought my wife might leave me if I failed to provide for her.

I felt the weight of the world on my shoulders. I felt alone. I felt scared to make a mistake, scared to take risks at work because I didn't want to be wrong. I felt angry that the economy was this way. What was our company thinking, letting people go and not talking about it? The crash was inevitable, and I felt furious that the little guys were affected by big policy decisions. I felt out of control. I feared that my life would be turned upside down if I didn't perform perfectly. I felt like a rat in a race, a pawn in a game, a piece of trash. I couldn't control what was happening, but it was my fault if I failed. I was scared out of my mind daily for 12 months.

I did act scared. I wouldn't talk to others at work. If projects had to be turned in, I would never hand them over when my supervisor was there. I would come early or stay late to put it on their desk. If possible, I would email it so I never had to look anyone in the eye. I used to be on the company ball team, but quit because I didn't want performance on the field to affect my standing in the office. I didn't take any risks. I never tried to think outside the box to improve assignments because I didn't want to have a different opinion and stand out. If I stood out, I might be let go. I tried to blend in and go unnoticed. I took all my frustration out after work. If my kids needed help with homework, I deferred to their mother. If my wife asked me to mow the lawn, I resisted. I stopped going to extended family reunions and neighborhood gatherings. I faked my way through all the conversations, knowing I was the only one who might lose his house. I stopped connecting with other people, especially the very ones I wanted to be closest to. My wife and I hadn't been intimate in months. I didn't know anything about what was going on in my kids' lives, who their friends were, how their grades were. I was barely keeping my head above water, giving the minimum effort possible in every arena of my life.

Consciousness

Being conscious is being present to where you have previously been, where you are presently and where you can possibly go. Our eyes are open to our efforts, to how they hurt or help us, to how they hurt or help others. We can look at our previous experiences and see our choices that we made way back when we were who we used to be. And we are okay with those choices. We accept the effort we were giving back then. We allow ourselves to progress on the learning curve that we are choosing. We aren't disappointed in ourselves or in our effort because we are trying our best. And if we realize that we need to increase our effort, we do it. We try our best to be aware of what we are choosing now and we accept the choices we make right now. We open our eyes to the possibilities that we can choose ahead of us. And we look forward to changing from a place of worth and acceptance.

We extend the same courtesy to others, accepting their past efforts and acknowledging their right to choose to change. We don't pigeon-hole people into categories because of previous experiences. We are okay with their choices because their choices make perfect sense, just like ours do. We can seek understanding on our own or courageously invest in our relationship with them to find out what is happening for them that we don't understand.

Consciousness means being aware of where we were, where we are and where we could possibly be. It also includes being satisfied with each of those locations. It's like pulling out old yearbook photos. You place them in a line side by side, so you can see your progression. And you mentally imagine yourself in the future. Your kindergarten photo is adorable—those curls, those dimples. Your fourth-grade shot, you could wonder what your mother was thinking, letting you choose your own outfit. You could wonder why you had a perm in your hair, why there are neon shoelaces adorning your hair clip, why there is paint on your t-shirt…on purpose, not by some accidental catastrophe. But you don't. Those were the times. That was the style. That's exactly how you should have looked. You look perfect. You are worthy and accepted no matter what because that was then. This is now and moving forward, you get to choose.

Consciousness is knowing what is going on and being okay with it. You're not embarrassed or ashamed because you know you were trying your best and if you weren't, you know you can change. You are enough.

You are conscious when you look at your previous experience and determine what you were experiencing. What did you think, feel and do? What is your present experience? What do you think, feel and do now? What is possible? Additionally, can you be satisfied with your choices previous, present and possible?

Consciousness also extends to our experience with others. We can look at our previous experiences with them and figure out what they possibly were thinking, feeling and doing? We can be satisfied with their efforts in the past and present as well. Consciousness is this satisfied awareness of things as they were and as they are and how they could be.

PLAY 10: CONSCIOUS

Previous	**Present**	**Possible**
Protect	**Experience**	Progress
HEAD ——————	**CHOOSE** ——————	**HEART**
Think	Think	Think
_____	_____	_____
Feel	Feel	Feel
_____	_____	_____
Do	Do	Do
_____	_____	_____

CHANGE – CONSCIENCE – COURAGE

Take a moment to become present to a previous experience and use this play. Choose an experience where you know you have seen yourself change. Write out your answers to these questions.

Where were you? What did you previously think, feel and do?

Where are you? What do you presently think, feel and do?

Where could you be? What could you possibly think, feel and do?

Join the **www.5Habits.me** community to see what others are experiencing for Play 10.

CHAPTER 11

Present Experience
Be Present to What You Experience

"Have you ever tried to change another person? How did that work for you? Did that person hear, understand and magically start doing things your way? Or did you become frustrated, irritable and angry at their inattention to your plan for how they should behave? Have you ever tried to change something about yourself that was out of your control? I have. It was fruitless. I decided to make peace with what I couldn't change, and it instantly made my life better!"
~Marshall Goldsmith

To go from our head to our heart—into the realm of possibility—we must become present to what we are experiencing, listen to our conscience and have the courage to act in accordance with it to create change.

For example, have you ever walked down a hall by yourself when out of nowhere comes another person? As he gets closer, the situation starts to get uncomfortable.

While trying to decide what to do, you start to think, "Should I look at them or not? If I look at them that may be weird or they may think I am weird. If I don't look at them, that would be rude. What will they think of me?"

Such thoughts may cause you to feel embarrassed, shy, self-conscious or nervous. So what you do is... look down, don't acknowledge them, pull out your phone and pretend you got a text or move away from them. We treat them as if they are a raptor about to attack us and we need to protect ourselves.

If you were totally in your heart you might think, "It's someone like me. They are probably worried about what I think of them. They seem nice."

I remember what I used to choose to think passing people in the hall. If they look up I will say hello. So you feel at ease, your normal self, compassion for them, an interest in connecting with them.

So what you do is say *hello*. Leave them space if they don't want to talk. Be normal, not uncomfortable and awkward. In this way, you are being respectful and being your best to choose your experience. We have a choice. We just have been doing things for so long in a certain way we had no idea what we were choosing.

When we go from our head to our heart often enough, we experience what we think, feel and do in the present. We have the courage to choose to change what we think, feel and do through conscious creation. We turn a previous experience into a new possibility. Even when we remember previous experiences where we did not follow our conscience, we get to change what we experienced by consciously creating a new experience.

We no longer have to work on becoming present because we are conscious of our previous experience as well as conscious of what is possible.

We do this by using our imagination and intelligence. Our intelligence is the left part of our brain that understands how things work and why they work. We can use it to make sense of what we are experiencing. When things make sense we can then accept them. It is difficult to accept something you don't understand. We are then conscious of what we are experiencing, giving us the ability to choose. Our imagination is the right part of our brain and it sees what is possible. It sees what we could be experiencing. Our left-brain or **intelligence** is more logical, analytical and objective while our right-brain or **imagination** is intuitive, thoughtful and subjective.

When we look at ourselves and others in terms of what we could possibly be, we realize the worth of people regardless of what they have experienced.

We can then create what we are experiencing, enabling us to choose. You can do this process over and over until it becomes part of you. You ask yourself questions and listen to your conscience to receive the answers. You will know what to do to change because you are ready to change. You know what to do to have courage because you are ready to have courage.

You will not be afraid of the answers because you know you are worthy and accepted. You will not just know the truth that you are worthy and accepted—you will experience it.

You will have the courage to overcome any challenge placed before you. You will love these challenges and experience progression. You will know that you are not alone and nothing is wrong with you. Your experiences are for a reason. And you do not have to accept your experience but rather you are the creator of what you experience.

You will know you are worthy of experiencing all that is good in life. You will accept where you are at in the current phase of your journey because you are present. You will go from wherever you are now to the next level, recognizing that is how we progress.

You can answer the question *why I am here?* Because you know: *where you are now, where you have been* and *where you are going.* You will understand that you are here to have experiences where you choose to go from your head to your heart. You will know that all these experiences are for your good because they enable you to choose to go from comfort and control to conscious creation. This is the refining process of discovering and being who you truly are. You are accountable, but not afraid. You will no longer do what you do to please others but will listen to your conscience.

Understanding your conscience is the most rewarding and satisfying experience because it sets you free, as the truth always does. You will be like a courageous lion.

Lion = Rebelling against your head (comfort/control) leading from your heart—using imagination and intelligence to consciously create what you experience in order to feel worthy and accepted

Others may see you as a rebel, not following the rules of the game.

Rebel = To choose not to follow the previous way of doing things

You will show others how to consciously create their own rules and they will follow you. This is not a new way to think. This is not a new way to feel. This is not a new thing to do. It has been within you all of your life and you have been doing it. You experienced it fully as a child. You have known there is more. You have known you were meant for more. Now is your time to become again like you were as a child. To choose your experience and create your restoration. Now is your time to courageously rebel.

Sometimes to gain freedom, you must choose rebellion.

What will you choose?

Christine: I love thinking for myself, being different from others. I choose to rebel.

PLAY 11: BE PRESENT—SEE AND SAY THE TRUTH

A simple way of describing the head-to-heart process or *being present* is seeing and saying the truth: what am I experiencing right now is…(head). The truth is…(heart).

So to practice this play, an example could be to revisit the same boss experience, but this time, express the truth. For example, you might say, "The truth is … I love my job. The truth is that I am really good at what I do and I get paid well for it. The truth is that my boss cares about more than just what I produce for his bottom line. The truth is that I am working hard, and sometimes I don't meet my expectations for myself. The truth is that sometimes I don't meet others' expectations for me. The truth is that I am reliable and I can try again if I mess up. The truth is that I have much to be grateful for. The truth is I am worthy, I am accepted, I am being my best self."

What is the truth as you see it? Write it down right now. What if you had a place that you could record the thoughts that bring you feelings of contentment and peace with yourself? What if you could read back through times in the past where the truth helped you? What if you were feasting on truth, pointing it out as you see it and recording it and reliving it by reading back through it? It would be no ordinary notebook or journal. Writing in a *Truth Journal* could be a powerful way to stay in your heart.

Write on the diagram an experience where you can see the truth. Write on the left column what you were experiencing and on the right hand column, write what the truth is instead.

Previous	**Present**	**Possible**
Protect	**Experience**	Progress
HEAD ——	**CHOOSE** ——	**HEART**

CHANGE – CONSCIENCE – COURAGE

Join the *www.5Habits.me* community to see what others are experiencing for Play 11.

CHAPTER 12

Possible Experience
You Can Now Create New Possibilities

"When our brains get stuck in a pattern that focuses on stress and negativity, we set ourselves up to fail. The brain can be trained to use a specific pattern for evaluating the environment (Tetris Effect). We thus retrain our brains to spot patterns of possibility and to see and seize opportunities wherever we look."

~Shawn Achor

To create a new possibility from a previous or present experience, you must become conscious of a time where you were in your head and use your heart to heal by creating a new experience.

Respond to Four Questions

Recall a time where you were not being respectful or not being your best self. Write your responses to these four questions—and don't leave any emotion behind (emotions are not good or bad—they simply help you realize you want to change):

What was your experience?
What were you thinking?
What were you feeling?
What did you do?

After you've recorded all aspects of being in your head using fight/flight and comfort/control, you can revisit the entire experience from your heart using your imagination and intelligence.

What could you be thinking?
What could you be feeling?
What could you do?

Explore Possibilities

Even though you are not changing the experience you are changing what you experience. What could you have experienced if you had been in your heart? What could you have been thinking, had you been present, following your conscience, being respectful of others, being your best self, accepting the best efforts of others? With your new thoughts, what could you have been feeling? With your new feelings, what could you do differently?

You have just chosen what you experience, no matter what experience happened to you. You are present.

There is no difference between an experience you are working through from a minute ago or 10 years ago. They are previous experiences where you get to choose your experience by going from your head to your heart.

Engaging in the process of conscious creation is so painful if you believe that there are only good and bad emotions. I am not saying that you want to feel angry and sad all the time, but you may need to feel these emotions in order to change.

If you feel angry or sad, you can recognize that your conscience is telling you that the experience you are choosing is causing you pain. Use your emotions as indicators of what you are choosing. You can then ask yourself questions about what you are choosing to experience, ensuring that you are choosing your experience instead of letting your previous experience choose for you.

You might ask yourself questions, such as: when I had that experience when I was being in my head, *what was I thinking? What was I feeling? What did I do?*

Once conscious of what you choose to experience, you can choose to consciously create a new experience by asking different questions:

If I were present and being in my heart, *what could I choose to think? What could I then feel? What could I then do?*

Asking such questions opens up new possibilities. It changes what we will do next time. It starts the process of healing by listening to our conscience.

This process happens naturally over time. We experience hurt over and over again until we choose a new experience. Think of experiences that used to bother you years ago, but no longer bother you. The head-to-heart framework enables you to eliminate the pain the first time you recognize it, rather than reliving it over years of experience.

Healing Wounds

This can be either a fast process or a slow one. If our patterns of not being present have built up for years, it may take time because of our choices over time. Just as our bodies store fat over time to protect us if we run out of food, we protect ourselves by storing experiences that keep us from being present so that no one can get close to us or hurt us.

Shedding the layers of protection we have built up is hard work because thinking, feeling and doing things about previous experience that hurt ourselves and others feels horrible. We bring up experiences so that we choose to be in our head and feel what we felt when we had the experience. This enables us to expel the poison, which is painful. We cover it up to keep functioning. This is the process of uncovering it, feeling it again and getting it out. These experiences are painful because we are healing the previous experience by getting the poison out. But we feel much better when we do what it takes to get the poison out.

When we work through these experiences, we no longer have that pain. Then what we think, feel and do about that experience is as if we were in our heart during the experience. We are no longer carrying around painful emotion based on thoughts that are not true. We have healed that experience leading from our heart. This is not pretending we did not have poisonous experiences. Poisonous experiences do happen. But what we think about ourselves and others while in our head, in fight/flight mode, does not have to keep poisoning us. We can heal from the poisonous thoughts we feed ourselves that are not true.

For example, if you cut your arm and the wound becomes infected, you must choose to leave it infected and hope it heals or do the work to clean it out. If you leave it infected, you do not have the pain of cleaning it out but the pain of infection remains.

After the intense pain of cleansing the wound, your body will have a clean environment in which to heal. You just get to choose if your pain has a purpose or not. Going from our head to our heart is painful in the short term, but in the long term we are healed.

You choose your experience by leading from your heart. You get out of your fight/flight pattern that prompts you to feel wrong and alone and to seek control or comfort. You tap into your imagination and intelligence, informed by your educated conscience, and you feel worthy and accepted—feelings that facilitate courageous action and conscious creation.

CHOOSE to be in Your HEART

The Boss Experience continues. . .

If I were totally in my heart when my boss walked in my office that Friday at 4 p.m., what could I think, feel and do?

Think: If I were totally in my heart I could have thought that he meant what he said. "Ready for the weekend?" I could have thought, "I can't wait." I could have thought about the other times he had walked into my office. He had usually had something on his mind and we were good brainstorming partners. I could have thought that he was reaching out to me for a brainstorming session—one of the things he said I was good at in our last employee performance evaluation. I could have thought about how ready he was for the weekend. He had twin boys on the high school baseball team who played every Friday night. I could have thought of the company culture he tried to create, encouraging all of us to move our work schedules to support our families when we needed to. I could have thought about my track record—I had never missed a report before. I could have thought of him as a person and not as a raptor.

Feel: I could have felt safe in my position and confident in the effort I was giving at work. I could have felt ready to receive criticism or feedback on how I could improve, knowing that my boss wasn't trying to demoralize me. I could have felt proud of everything I had accomplished that week, despite the missing report. I could have felt flattered that my boss had taken time to come in and chat with me, finding out how things were going for me. I could have felt grateful for this new job. I could have felt connected to my boss.

Do: I could have acted accountable and told him that I didn't have the report finished. I could have asked him if it was a priority for him before he left for the night or if it could wait for Monday. I could have asked him about his projects, his meeting with corporate or his family.

Power to Choose

Why do we stay in *wrong and alone*, even when the play hurts us? Again, something has happened to you, you form a thought about it and your conscience sends you a message. One of the reasons we explode into action after strong feelings we receive is because we are not simply feeling what's happening in that exact moment.

Your mind and body have recorded when you've felt that feeling your entire life. And what if you have never been taught to let go of the thought associated with that feeling? That means when that feeling comes up again, it continues to come up in a ferocious way because you're not simply dealing with what's going on in that moment. You're feeling the intensity of many previous experiences that have never been restored.

It's like shaking a can of soda. You can shake it and shake it and nothing happens until eventually the soda can explodes by itself. It didn't need anyone to pop it open because it is an automatic reaction that can't be stopped. Your power to choose increases as you discover what previous experiences are holding you back. For example, consider some feelings you might have if this situation happened to you. Your mother-in-law disapproves of a decision you make. Here are some feelings that might accompany that experience.

Feel: I feel annoyed. I feel angry. I feel judged. I feel like I'm never going to do it right, so why try? I feel trapped. I feel like no matter what I do, I'm wrong.

Think about a time when you have felt misjudged. You can heal your wound of misjudgment by figuring out when else you have felt misjudged. When have you previously felt the pain of being misjudged? Feelings are identifiable because the emotion can be strong. Feelings can help us identify which thoughts are not serving us well. Examine what thoughts preceded your previous feeling. Then you can courageously think of other possible ways to think, feel and act for that experience that has already happened.

Previous Feeling – I have felt judged by my mother-in-law before, that's for sure.

Previous Thoughts – I think she never really liked me or wanted me to marry her daughter. I think she didn't think I was good enough. I think I won't ever get an equal return on investment for my relationship with her.

Previous Do: I have always held back from reaching out to her. We moved away when we got a job offer when we first married. It was definitely the right decision, but it wasn't hard for me like it was for my wife when we were deciding. I bristle at little things when I'm around her that I would never think twice about around my parents. Like if she doesn't say hello to me right away when we walk into the room. Or if she doesn't call me on my birthday like my parents call my wife. Or if she makes a joke out of something I said, I take it way too personally.

When I felt judged, I also felt wrong. I can see now how feeling wrong is my conscience's way of telling me that something is wrong, to examine my thoughts. So what possibly could have been happening was:

Possible Feelings: I could have felt nervous to join their family. I could have felt confident in their support of us. They were so patient with my wife while she was changing her mind every day about wedding plans. I could have felt the love they were trying to give me.

Possible Thoughts: I could have thought about what it felt like to be my parents-in-law or about how I was marrying their only daughter. If someone came to marry my little girl, I know I wouldn't handle that well. Come to think of it, they handled it so well! I would be polishing shotguns and chasing away suitors. Wow, they really love their daughter, just like I do.

Possible Do: I could have reached out to them more. I could have moved away for my job, looking forward to staying connected to them instead of relieved to have the distance. I could have tried harder.

Understand that your current experience is a compilation of all your previous experiences. These convert into wisdom when you learn what your conscience was telling you in those previous experiences. Now that you've created the power to choose, you can do this. You are not forced to react when the same feelings arise again because now you have the power. So, of all the choices that are available, what will you choose to think, feel and do?

PLAY 12: CHOOSE YOUR EXPERIENCE

Think of a strong feeling you have had previously. Write on the left hand column when you have felt that feeling before in other experiences. Figure out if your conscience was instructing you to have courage to change or continue. Write what you could possibly have thought, felt and done. And then, and only then, do. Your previous experiences have no power over you to force you to react. You get to freely choose your experience.

Previous	Present	Possible
Protect	**Experience**	Progress
HEAD ——	**CHOOSE** ——	**HEART**
		Think
Feel		**Feel**
		Do

CHANGE— CONSCIENCE — COURAGE

Join the *www.5Habits.me* community to see what others are experiencing for Play 12.

HABIT 5

Be a Conscious Creator
Go from Principle to Personal Experience

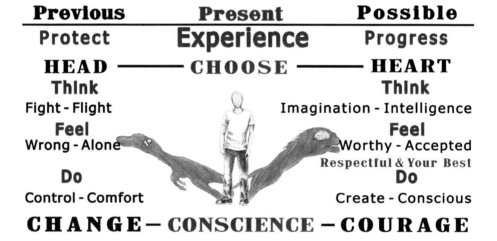

Previous	Present	Possible
Protect	**Experience**	Progress
HEAD ———	**CHOOSE** ———	**HEART**
Think		**Think**
Fight - Flight		Imagination - Intelligence
Feel		**Feel**
Wrong - Alone		Worthy - Accepted
		Respectful & Your Best
Do		**Do**
Control - Comfort		Create - Conscious

CHANGE — CONSCIENCE — COURAGE

Being a Conscious Creator is the result of experiencing all 5 habits.

The raptor represents who we choose to be while in our head. We use the protecting part of our brain as shown in the raptor, to resist change. We protect ourselves through control and comfort. The lion represents who we choose to be while in our heart. We use the progressing part of our brain as shown in the lion, to be courageous. We progress ourselves as a conscious creator.

Habit 5 uses the fifth phase of the head-to-heart framework as shown above.

In habit 5, we will learn to choose to become conscious creators. This is the *do* habit.

From history, we know that many of the men and women who were conscious creators, such as our founding fathers, were seen as **rebels** (indeed, they often led rebellions).

When we personally experience something, we can then *consciously create* that experience again. When I say consciously create, I mean anything that comes from you. In the movie "It's a Wonderful Life," Jimmy Stewart, with the help of an angel, sees how different everything would be without his influence and presence in the world. That's what I'm suggesting: your creations are how you influence the world, and how you create is the way you do it.

This habit takes what you just experienced and opens up new ways to use the head-to-heart framework to consciously create new possibilities.

When you are being courageous, being you and present so you can restore yourself, you are being a conscious creator. Only when you are experiencing all of the first four habits of the heart, can you be consciously creating. This book is a culmination of five years full-time conscious creation of thinking, writing, applying and teaching these principles.

There were many years that have led up to it, but the last five years were steadily increasing my ability to consciously create. Conscious creation takes a lot of preparation to get to and often does not last very long. It is mostly laying the groundwork so that when the time is right, the experiences are aligned so that something amazing can happen.

There are many amazing experiences along the way of creating this book and the head-to-heart framework, yet looking back, it looks like a thousand small steps. Each step in the moment feels amazing and is a breakthrough yet only moved me and this work forward one step. The beauty is that each step is so satisfying and not the end of the journey.

The end is never as great as you think it should be. Think about a movie during the last few minutes. It may be the peak of engagement and the most thrilling, but soon the credits are rolling and the suspense is gone. Conscious creation is how we progress. It is being present to what we were previously experiencing and could possibly experience and taking that next step. Now is your time to take the next step, regardless of how big or small.

CHAPTER 13

Conscious Creation
Personal, Relationship and Group

"The transition from the Reactive to the Creative Mind is arduous—only about 20% of us ever make this so-called Hero's Journey. It is not for the faint of heart."
~Bob Anderson

This fifth habit is focused on the *do,* or execution. This is my wife's favorite part. I can hear her now, "Can we stop talking about our Saturday chores so we can just get them done?" Until now I have focused on changing how you think and feel because once your thoughts and feelings change, your actions will naturally follow. Now, let's do what we have been talking about.

The action is where all of this goes from practice and principles to personal experience. Personal experience cements everything into place, making it a natural and permanent part of how you live. This is why we focus so much on changing what we are doing because personal experience makes what we think and feel about it personal.

When we are in our heart we are consciously creating. We are using our left and right brain to feel worthy and accepted, allowing us to do what we choose to do. We are not confined to the rut of what we have previously done. We are not robotically performing what we are expected to do. But we are conscious of the possibilities and able to create those possibilities.

Three Levels of Conscious Creation

As you expand your capacity to be conscious, you can create three levels of conscious creation:

1) *personal,* where you are experiencing it by yourself; 2) in a *relationship,* where you experience with one other person and 3) in a *group,* where you experience it with two or more other people. You might rate yourself on a scale of 1 to 7 where you are in each level so you can take the next step. What I say about each level also applies to the other levels, simply because you are part of each level. So use what you learn in one area on any area of your life.

In this chapter, I will cover the *personal* and *relationship* levels and discuss the *group* level in the next chapter.

Level 1: Personal

Being *present* is difficult because life never stops. So, being present is not something you can check off your list. You must intentionally choose to be present all the time. Life takes us from one extreme to the other. Being present is the goal, even though we will never be present 100% of the time. We will swing on the pendulum—from aware and accountable to ignorant and irresponsible. When we are present, we are constantly examining ourselves. Am I being respectful? Am I being my best?

Being present means accepting our personal best effort. I'm not discouraged with where I am because it is enough. My best effort is enough. And we are constantly taking into account that others around us are usually trying their best. If they are disrespectful to us, they probably don't realize it. And if they do mean to be disrespectful, we can handle it. And we are only dealing with their disrespect in that moment because we've already let go of our previous experiences of being disrespected. So we can calmly and rationally talk to someone who is being disrespectful. Being present is the most accountable and hands-on way to live. It's hard work, but promotes progress. And this progress, moving forward, ever learning, feels so good.

Using the head-to-heart framework helps us to become present. It's not 10 different exercises—it is doing that same process over and over. What shifts is the experience or problem or circumstance you focus on. You shift from head to heart in the area you focus on. When you are in your heart, you are using your imagination and intelligence (your right and left brain, or neocortex) to consciously create what you experience.

Imagination and Intelligence

To become a conscious creator, we need to exercise our imagination and intelligence.

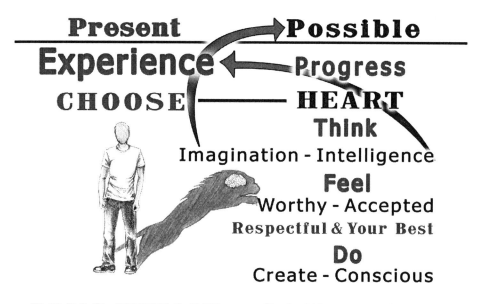

Imagination is the ability to see possibility. When we listen to our conscience instructing us to have courage to continue, we might not be available to move forward. We could be too tired or have too many commitments. But if we are available to move forward, imagination is an incredible place to be. It usually leaves you feeling more worthy and more accepted because you worked out an authentic win-win. You had courage to move into the unknown and find out what would work. Imagination is one of my favorites because it involves finding the 3ʳᵈ alternative.

For example, imagine that your 10-year-old son wants the latest and greatest video game. He brings it up a few times daily. All of his friends have the game, and he wants it too.

What are you experiencing?

Think: you think he is obsessing over this game. You think that might be a good thing because you could use it for leverage with homework time. You think he is such a good kid with lots of talents. You think he might be at his current limit for screen time. You think several parents in the neighborhood spoil their kids. You don't want your child to be spoiled, but you do want him to have a great life.

Feel: you feel annoyed at his singular focus. Why can't he focus on something more productive? You feel proud because focus is a skill he will need to succeed. You feel hesitant because you definitely don't want to be in the race against the Jones'. You know you will never win on your single parent salary. You feel rested enough to take the time to figure it out with him. You can honestly say that you are okay with whatever solution you come up with together.

Do: you tell your son that you want to sit down and talk to figure out this video game. His head immediately drops because he thinks that is code for *dream on*. You laugh and ask him if he is available to brainstorm a solution. Your conversation goes like this:

"Tell me about this video game."

"It's so awesome! I tried it at Matt's house. I can already make it to Level 2 on my own."

"May I share with you some of my concerns about getting this new game?"

"Sure."

"First, is it violent? I don't like it when you're plugged into violent games. I think you treat others around you with disrespect when you're constantly playing violent video games."

"Well, you definitely have to defeat the villain at the end, but it's not like that guns and ammo game we got rid of a few weeks ago. I don't think it's too violent."

"Remember the game that I bought you a few weeks ago? I had no idea it was so gruesome, and I wasted my money on it. I definitely don't want to make that mistake again."

"Right. Matt's mom would let you see it, and you can tell it's not a violent game."

"My second concern is that you will play it and forget about all of your other responsibilities. Homework and chores still need to be done well in order to have screen time."

"I promise I will do my homework and get all my jobs done."

"My third concern is that after you've beaten the game, it will go into the pile of games you never play anymore. What could we do about that?"

"Well, I don't know. I probably should sell my old games that I don't use anymore right now and that could help pay for this new game."

"That sounds like a great idea to me. Then I'm not investing anything new into this and you're committed to keep your school and house commitments when you get the game. Thanks for listening to all of my concerns. That helps me want to figure things out with you instead of just saying *No* all the time. We are such a good team!"

Intelligence is the ability to understand experience. Intelligence is powerful because you understand what is happening, while it is happening. And you can look back on previous experiences to understand what was really happening. Intelligence is a time-saving play. When you use your intelligence to understand what is going on, you avoid so much pain. Experiences hurt us over and over until we change the way we think about them so we don't feel the painful feelings anymore. Intelligence gets you past the pain. You intelligently refrain from choosing thoughts that hold you back. You intelligently avoid being hurt by intended and imagined offenses. Intelligence is powerful because you allow yourself to move forward with understanding. Without intelligence, misunderstandings multiply, relationships are ruined, neighborhoods are divided and countries go to war.

During our experiences, we can ask intelligent questions, including: do I understand that I am worthy and accepted? Am I allowing others to be worthy and accepted? Do I understand what is happening? What does it mean? What does it not mean? What could it possibly mean? Is my conscience giving me instructions to change or have courage to continue? Am I ready to change or have courage to continue right now?

Intelligence does not eliminate negative thoughts. They exist and serve their purpose. Intelligence enables you to sift and sort, to understand what is really happening and work through what you are experiencing so that you maintain your power to choose.

Consider the following example. You are out to eat as a family. Everyone is settling in with their plates of food piled high from the buffet. Your 10-year-old boy is a little ambitious carrying soda, dessert and entrée at the same time as he maneuvers down the crowded aisle to your table in the back. Just as you are about to voice a word of caution, the inevitable happens: soda hits the floor, almost splashing the table next to you. Mashed potatoes are splattered everywhere. The ice cream sundae is all over him.

Think: I think that this is ridiculous! He always bites off more than he can chew. How embarrassing! I can't take these people anywhere without a freak show happening.

Feel: I feel frustrated and embarrassed.

Do: Nothing.

In this moment, try to go back to think some more.

Think: Do I understand that I am worthy and accepted? Yes, my value is not based on my child making a mess. I'm not going to get kicked out of the restaurant for spilling. I can ask our server for help.

Am I allowing my child to be worthy and accepted? Yes, my child's value is not based on if he makes a mistake or not. This is embarrassing but we can move forward and learn from this. As his parent, I can help him learn without trying to make him feel wrong and alone.

Do I understand what is happening? Yes, my 10-year-old was holding too much food at once and he spilled his food. *What does that mean?* It means he was holding too much food at once and he spilled his food. *What does it not mean?* It does not mean that he's a bad kid or that he should be punished or that he did it on purpose. *What could it possibly mean?* It could mean that he was trying to save time and consolidate trips. It could mean that he's extremely hungry and excited to eat. It could mean that I didn't give my kids instructions about this restaurant before we came. It could mean that he's trying his best and accidents happen. *Is my conscience giving me instructions to change or have courage to continue?* I feel like I can change. I can help my child understand that accidents happen and he can help the waiter clean up his mess.

Am I ready to change right now? Yes, I am.

Feel: I feel love for my child. I feel accountable for the fact I should have warned him about how many plates to carry. I feel compassion and connection with him because I have definitely done embarrassing things before.

Do: I go over to my son and smile. I go with him to find the waiter so we can help clean it up together. I ask him what he's going to fill his next plate with.

Intelligence sounds like it takes a lot of time to think through, but it doesn't. These thoughts are shooting through our minds at warp speed. What it requires is practicing this play. Ask yourself if you understand what you are experiencing. Start with simple things so that you can work up to things that are harder for you. Intelligence will help you to eliminate the pain you are choosing in your life. Things hurt until you choose to not let them hurt anymore. The way to choose is to be intelligent: understand your experiences.

In the space between relinquishing control and not being comfortable, you can consciously create something new that enables you to have what you really want—to feel worthy and accepted. In this creative state, you no longer see yourself as bad or feel that you should be somebody else or somewhere else—you are open to the possibility to choose something different. This is respecting where you are now and accepting your best effort.

When you do this, you are ready to become present. You are ready to go from your head to your heart. Making this change will be challenging because you need to change what you think and feel in order to do what you need to do. And breaking a pattern you have previously lived for years can cause pain. This pain comes from not listening to our conscience. When our conscience tells us to change, but we do not change, we will keep feeling that pain of wrong and alone until we do change.

When the body feels pain and tells us to change, we may try to numb the pain with food, drugs and other behaviors or distractions, just as we try and numb ourselves by not thinking or feeling. The reason these thoughts and feelings of wrong and alone come to us is to prompt us to change. The pain is telling us to change.

To change we must be present to what we are experiencing and dispel our poisonous thoughts. This will stop the feelings of being wrong and alone.

Our feelings are a reaction to what we are thinking, just as the pain of touching a hot stove is a reaction from our nervous system. Think of our emotions as messengers from our conscience, telling us to get the poison out. When we eat too much or eat something that has gone bad, our stomachs tell us to stop eating or get out the food. We feel sick telling us to change so we will think and do something different.

When we feel wrong and/or alone, our emotions tell us to get the thought out. We change what we are feeling by processing or metaphorically vomiting the thoughts out. Although it doesn't feel good during the process, both systems are doing their jobs perfectly.

The way we try and change our emotions is by holding them in by controlling them to not feel them or seek comfort in order to avoid feeling them for a moment.

We have focused so many years as a society on just doing something different. We often do not stop to consider what we do is based on what we think and what we feel.

What we think and feel is a matter of whether or not we are following our conscience. We follow our conscience by leading from our heart and by following the three ground rules—be respectful, be your best and be present. When we respect ourselves and others we feel of worth. When we are being our best selves and let others be their best selves, we feel accepting of ourselves and others, regardless of where we are or where they are in life. When we are not being respectful or being our best, we can choose to be present to what we are experiencing in our head so we can choose to go back into our heart.

In our heart, when we know there is a problem, we work on it. We don't agonize over the fact that it took us so long to see the problem or that we chose to create the problem. We choose what we are experiencing regardless of the experience.

Conscious creation represents a change in what we experience. We use our intelligence to become conscious of what we are experiencing and what we could possibly do. We use our imagination to create something we have only seen as a possibility. We do what we once thought or felt we could never do.

Conscious creation takes courage because we must step into the unknown. It is uncomfortable when we don't have complete control. We don't know if it will work or not. It may feel like our previous experience of being wrong.

Moreover, we don't know what others will think. And that feels like our previous experience of being alone.

Pondering and Pen Pondering

One big barrier to conscious creation is that other people are often scared because of how our change will affect them. I see two effective ways to address this barrier: *pondering* and *pen pondering.*

Pondering is using your mind to think through your experience. I love pondering. My four-year-old son and I ponder the same way. You can always tell when I'm deep in thought because I'm picking at my nails–fingernails or toenails. I sit and stare into space. And my fingers go to work to pull off any stray pieces of skin that didn't get clipped properly. All the while, I'm computing, digesting and pondering about something that's on my mind.

Pen pondering is using your mind by putting pen to paper to think through your experience. Pen pondering is great because no one is grading your paper. You are not writing to please someone else. If you are hesitant to pen ponder, you are thinking way too hard about it.

When my wife is really angry, she writes line on top of line on top of line until it's completely illegible. She says she knows that her thoughts are irrational, so she doesn't want anyone to read them. But there is still purpose to *writing it out* to *get it out.* You just let it flow. If you're stuck, you can make it simple. Write your name. Ask yourself a question. Then start writing about what you think or feel about something. Then let it all spill out onto the page. Isn't that the way relationships work? You start on the surface, and eventually you work your way down to the important stuff.

With both pondering and pen pondering, you use the head-to-heart framework to ask yourself questions after an experience. "Okay, what am I thinking, feeling and doing? My conscience has told me to change because this is not feeling good. I will listen to my feelings as indicators from my conscience that something is not working, and I can change it. So, now what can I possibly think, feel and do in my heart? What do I have the courage to do?" **This is how you choose your experience!**

Whether it's a previous or present experience, you can always *ponder* or *pen ponder*, "What's going on? Why am I feeling this way? What am I experiencing?" When you listen to your conscience, you gain the empathy to understand why other people do what they choose to do, "When they did that, I took it to mean this and I felt this. Instead, what could they have possibly been thinking, feeling and doing?" You can then take the next step, shifting from your head to heart in choosing your response and your experience.

Over time, this head-to-heart process becomes semi-automatic. You choose wisely what you experience, instead of robotically reacting to whatever comes your way. It is this simple. The hard part is becoming present and doing the process over and over.

Doing happens first in your mind's eye. The mind's eye is what we use to see things using our mind. When we are in our heads and repeating the same experience over and over in our mind's eye, it goes from experiencing it one time to thousands of times. This is the same for experiences in our heart. We can repeat the experience over and over.

To use our heart to do this is usually something we must focus on in order to choose it. With our head, we choose to replay the experience almost automatically. We need to develop the ability to become present and then choose what we experience. We start by recognizing what we are experiencing, and then we choose a new experience.

When your conscience sends a feeling as a messenger telling you to change, you can become present and choose your experience. Your sensitivity will increase over time so you will have multiple times a day to practice this process as you play the game of your life.

Find plays that help you to do what you know you should do. Essentially, all good plays will take you through the head-to-heart process. Now that you know the process, you can use it to work through the thoughts you have that keep you from applying the plays. You recognize what you are feeling and what those feelings are telling you so you can move forward to use the tool in a way that works for you. As a result, you will do something that brings you peace. The head-to-heart process is how to get where you want to be.

If you don't have a way to feel and express your emotions, seriously consider starting one. Suppose that you don't express anything, anytime to anyone. Think of the activities you're engaging in purposefully to avoid feeling. Think of repetitive, mindless behaviors that you use as an escape, but you don't feel invigorated afterwards. Avoiding your feelings means avoiding the messages your conscience is trying to send to you. And your conscience is the entity that leads you to peace, to what's best for you. Think of emotional expressions you've seen: teenagers rolling their eyes? It's a not-so-polite way to feel emotion, express it and move on. Next time you get the eye roll, congratulate your teenager for expressing emotions.

How to Do What You Know You Should Do

To help you do what you know you should do, you might seek a *mentor* who has mapped out the specifics in the areas you want to experience. For example, if you want to experience more peace, you might use the tool of meditation. You likely already use some meditative practice in your life. Do you ride a bike to get away from it all? Sing in the shower just for fun? Go for a run to think things over? There are healthy ways to feel what you're supposed to feel.

Here are the four most common ways to do what you know you should do:

1. *Questioning* is one way to find out what you should do. I encourage you to make your own list of questions—ones that work for you. It won't be the same every time. Questioning is great because it brings you step-by-step closer to your answer. And steps forward are somewhat measurable, even though you are progressing toward immeasurable ends like peace, happiness, contentment. So, in an attempt to move measurably forward towards the immeasurables, here are some sample questions.

Feel an emotion.

✓ Ask: *what is this emotion telling me? Should I have courage to continue or change?*

✓ Ask: *what thought is connected to this emotion? Should I keep my thought or can I replace my thought with the truth?*

✓ Ask: *when have I previously had that thought or emotion? What was really happening in my previous experience?*

✓ Ask: *could I choose to experience something different?*

Choose your experience.

Do this every single time. Every day. Multiple times a day. Questioning helps you find the courage to change or to continue.

2. Writing is the best tool for expressing how you feel. It is simple and universal. It takes your thoughts and feelings from looping over and over in your mind to something concrete. You can do something about it once you get it all out. Your ability to clarify your thoughts and feelings is critical in becoming present and choosing your experience. When you can shift from just doing it in your mind to doing it on paper, you find that there is magic in the actual pen to paper. The physical act of bringing together your thoughts and writing them out pulls together your left and right hemispheres of your brain so you are fully engaged.

This is not to say that you need to do it on paper every time. When I want to become present to what I am experiencing, I start doing the process in my mind. If I am working through the previous experiences that led to my present experience and create a new possible experience, I write about it. This links a present experience to previous experiences and gets to the root. Putting it on paper enables me to know where I have been and where I am going. It is an intentional act to organize and make sense of our experiences.

Many people hate to write because they associate writing with deadlines and English classes and red marks. If you have had bad experiences writing, use the head-to-heart process to work through it. I have done this myself. Only my wife and I can read my handwriting. I had a hard time with school and my handwriting and spelling are still at a grade school level. Thank goodness for editors and spellcheck.

When we write more than when we type, we make a deeper connection. Writing taps into the creative side and it is a lot more personal. It's the difference between a hand-written note and a typed note—same words but different feeling.

You want to feel as you write in order to not just understand what you were previously experiencing and could possibly experience but to feel what you were previously experiencing and feel the new possibility. Your thoughts and feelings translate into what you do. If you tend to avoid your feelings, writing is the perfect way to get them out and sift through them. If you are not ready to write, you can type. I understand why you would do that. Your willingness to examine yourself is enough. It's perfect. It will work for you. In discovery mode, writing is a way to try different possibilities. You can explore without getting stuck down a particular path.

3. *Talking* is another way to change—it is simply verbally going through the same process. It naturally turns into a two-way conversation. This happens as we write or type. It's a way of discovering that helps us not be stuck on repeat and just go through the motions.

I do this often in the car, in my office and outside. It's what I do when I am in discovery mode, seeing something in a new way, or when I have already *pen pondered*. I know what I think about it, but I want to fully feel it. I seek emotion when I feel disconnected. If something is not coming together for me, I want to open up and feel so I can become connected to someone or to what's really going on. For example, I might be extremely upset about a relationship with someone. When I want to feel something and work through it, I can talk out loud. It is like I am having the experience in real life, except I am by myself because it would be disrespectful to have the person with me while I am exploring all of my feelings.

In our family, we call it the *passing gas* principle. We all need to expel excess gas out of our digestive system. We all need to do it, but it is disrespectful to pass gas in someone's face. So, I talk through it out loud and alone.

In addition, I want to be alone so I can fully be myself. I'm not worried about others' judgment of me as I fully express myself. When I am in my head, I need to get the emotions out before I can use my heart. So being angry, sad or mean without the person being there is better than doing it to them. Think of people who need to yell to feel better. They get their frustration out, which is a good thing, but what about the people who get yelled at? They have to experience all that frustration. Getting all of the emotion out, without passing gas in anyone's face, provides the same emotional release but does not do damage to the other person.

This doesn't mean that you stuff all of your emotions or thoughts away and have your own private volcanic eruptions. It is not so dramatic. By working through previous experiences, we don't need to do this clearing as often. Still, we are emotionally where we are. Just because we are adults does not mean we are not like children and have emotions that we need to get out.

This private emotional release does not make things perfect because you get all your emotions out. You still have the same conflict. You are just changing how you deal with it. Instead of reacting to something that happens, you pause. You take time to identify what you are feeling and thinking. You release any pent-up feelings or thoughts from previous experiences and then you can work on your conflict from your heart. You won't have pent-up or misplaced emotion for the current experience. You can calmly and rationally work through the conflict and create something that works for you.

For some people, it seems mean or rude to get mad at someone. They would rather pretend they are not mad. The problem is they are mad and become numb and are passive-aggressive to this person because they are ignoring them or are fake around them.

For others, emotional outbursts are how they get things done. They go along and pretend everything is just fine, until it isn't. An emotional explosion is how they communicate that something isn't working. Then others around them cower to them because they want to end or avoid that experience. Such *emotional terrorism* is not healthy, but it happens all the time. It's not just the obvious ranting and raving or tears streaming. Fight or flight mode also includes withdrawing, refusing to connect, giving the silent treatment. Just because we grow up doesn't mean that we have a higher proficiency with our emotions and how we use them.

Give yourself permission to feel what you are feeling without hurting others around you. Once you have let it out, use your heart, your imagination and intelligence, to find out why you were so mad. You can consciously create a solution so it stops happening. You will exercise the muscle of pausing, not reacting to everything around you.

When I want to feel an emotion that is positive, doing this alone works as well. Many people hold in both the good feelings and the bad. We don't want to be too mad or too happy. I know I do this. I am cautious about being too happy about something because what if it does not last? What if something happens? It's not that big of a deal.

We all do this because we all care what others think about us. Somewhere along the line, expressing emotion has been put in the *faux pas* category of how people should act. Adults are embarrassed to cry. It looks like weakness. Children are told to toughen up and shut up. This dehumanization can be reversed, if you try. You may need to practice being excited, happy or crazy by yourself before you do it in front of others.

I do this before dancing, making a presentation or telling someone how I feel about them. Often the next step must be experienced by ourselves before we are ready to courageously share it with others. Part of the reason we do this is because people can be as harsh about you being excited as they are about you being mad. Mad is a socially acceptable emotion because a group can thrive on being mad together. As long as you are not mad at them, collective anger is alright. But emotional discrepancies can divide people. If you are happy and they are not, they do not want to be left behind and will try and bring you back into the group emotion.

4. Go through the head-to-heart process in your mind. This is the most common way because we can do it anytime. The other techniques require more focus and time alone. But hopefully you use the time you have to use your mind to prepare to engage in other techniques.

All four of these ways to express yourself are helpful. See what works for you. Spend time doing it daily. Find times that you would usually try to distract yourself from being in your head and feeling. It could be listening to music, playing a game on your phone or getting on social media. Instead, consciously create what you experience. It will be challenging at first, but over time you will enjoy it and it will bring you great satisfaction. You will enjoy the challenge and you will think about it because you love the challenge and love to progress.

As you do these four things you become proficient at leading from your heart and following your conscience. Answers to *what should I do next* or *what is the best thing for me to do* will come to you. You will understand what really was happening when you had a previous experience come up for you. You will learn what you need to learn from that experience. We have the answer to our problems, we just need to know how to ask and ask again. And you can figure it out. You will receive answers internally and recognize what has been in front of your face the whole time. You will remember things you have not thought about for years. You will come across exactly what you are looking for. As you seek truth, you find it. If you are courageous enough to do the work, you get the reward. It is hard work and the peace you get is invaluable. Things hurt until…they don't hurt anymore.

So far I have focused mainly on thinking and feeling through these four ways. There are so many things to do that work. I will not name all of them, but rather give you some ideas so you can see what you are currently doing and what you could possibly do. For example, when we are in our head and want to change what we are experiencing we can: exercise, play, meditate, unplug and feel what we are feeling, call someone, sew, crossword, work on a puzzle or take a drive.

The purpose of doing something is to get out of the pattern of thinking that is causing pain. When we use our body to do a physical activity, we are engaged in less thinking and more doing. The more physically demanding the activity is, the more of a release we can feel. If we are angry it is easier to feel angry when you are pushing your body. If you are feeling sad, you can feel drained and fully feel sad when you are pushing your body.

When we are in our heart, we may do the same activities—exercise, play, unplug and feel what we are feeling, call someone, sew, crossword, work on a puzzle, take a drive. Everyone is different. As you think through what you do to go from your head to your heart, you will find a pattern. The key is to find the pattern that works for you and do it in a healthy way.

Level 2: Relationships

Our relationships, more than anything else, give us a chance to be present. By ourselves, we can pretend to be far better than we are. We can remain blind to our own character flaws. When we interact with others we see immediately where we are, what to change and when to have courage to continue. Relationships enable us to see what we couldn't see before. Relationships provide connection, which is important when we feel alone and wrong. Every aspect of relationships helps us to be present, aware of our effort and respectful.

The greatest joys and pains in life come from our relationships because in a relationship we open up and let someone in. That can feel good, and that can feel bad. When I talk about a *relationship*, I am talking about you connecting with another person. The deeper the relationship, the deeper the vulnerability and the joy or pain can be. If we apply the items in the personal sections to ourselves, our relationship will progress. Most of what we experience in our relationships is a reflection of what we are choosing to experience within ourselves. The relationship is the experience, but what we choose to experience within it is up to us.

This is why blaming the other person is so common. If I were to look within myself I would see I am the one who needs to change. I realize that I am the only one that I can do anything about. So much frustration comes from wanting someone else to be different.

I am the one who gets to choose. I am the one causing myself this pain. It is so much easier to blame someone else and try to control the situation. We gain control of relationships by making someone else wrong or seeking comfort by being alone. Here is where we can be present and accountable and powerful in every relationship we have.

I believe we can't be truly happy unless we first have a relationship with ourselves where we feel we are worthy and accepted. Then we are able to have relationships with others where they feel worthy and accepted by us. We can never really have a relationship that we both feel worthy and accepted beyond the level we feel worthy and accepted by ourselves.

We can feel another person is worthy and accepted far beyond how we experience worthiness and acceptance ourselves. However you cannot think that others feel you are worthy and accepted beyond where you feel you are. In your mind's eye, you can lift others above where you think you are, but you won't allow others to lift you above where you think you are. Have you had the experience of loving someone and regardless of how much you tell them you love them or how you would do anything for them, they cannot accept your love? They may accept that you love them but they cannot accept completely and fully be loved. This is because they personally do not feel worthy of your love and cannot accept it.

Our work is to personally participate in the head-to-heart process so that we allow others to share their love with us. And we can support them in participating in the head-to-heart process so they can do their work to feel worthy and accepted. Relationships with people who feel worthy and accepted are abundant, connected, considerate and caring. There is no backbiting or gossiping, comparison or criticism. The capacity to create is limitless.

There are effective ways to work through what you are experiencing together, ideally after each of you have done it individually.

If either of you are in your heads, I suggest you take a break and allow both of you to do your own work to get in your heart. When my wife and I do this we say to each other, "Let's talk about this when we can have a heart-to-heart." We do our best to not engage when we are in our heads. When we are having a head-to-head, we only say things that hurt each other and the conversation never moves forward. Heart-to-heart allows progress because each person is coming from a place of accountability, acknowledging we are each trying our best. Head-to-head for us means that someone is going to walk away a winner and someone is going to walk away as the loser. When you win by making someone else lose, it's not a real victory. When we are arguing and it is going nowhere, we make a plan to talk when we are willing and ready.

Sometimes we just need time. Our wounds are too fresh, but when we come back we can work through it quickly. If it is an ongoing concern or offense, we do our best to be in our heart and keep working at it until we can create a new perspective or solution. This does not mean we will never think and feel the same about it because we are continually working on it.

When either of us has been hurt by the other, we have a way to share what we are thinking and feeling. This allows us to share something, regardless of how big or how small it seems. A dear family friend shared this advice with us at the beginning of our marriage. She explained that you can easily bring things up without worrying about offending each other because you committed to following the rules. It's called the no-fester rule. Over time, any small issue can bubble up to become a big issue. It's much easier and less stressful to put the energy into talking about small things instead of waiting and having bigger problems on your hands.

When my wife was getting her Master's degree, she had a family relations class. As newlyweds, we would talk about all of the things she was learning. She told me that women are prone to *kitchen sink* their husbands. You may have experienced it already, as I have. *Kitchen sinking* is when someone brings up every poor choice you've ever made, including the kitchen sink. It's a great way to clear all of your previous experiences, but harmful because you're breaking the *no passing gas in someone's face* rule. And *kitchen sinking* could be avoided if you were following the no-fester rule. It's best to bring things up as they happen, without the ferocity of every previous experience behind it. Often the initial experience was not intended to hurt the other person but over time becomes a huge raptor.

This rule of feedback gives each person the opportunity to explain what they were thinking and feeling. Often when both sides understand the background information, there is no issue. The reason we want this understanding is so that we are always *crystal clear.*

Imagine every relationship you are in represented by a pane of glass, with each of you on opposite sides. You can clearly see the other person when the glass is clean. We flick mud on the glass when we are disrespectful or when we aren't trying our best. The mud clouds how we see that person as well as makes it unpleasant to look through the glass. *Crystal clear* means that when mud gets on the window, we only have two options. We wipe it off ourselves on our side of the glass. Or we have the courage to be honest to let them know they have some mud that needs to be wiped off on their side. Preventing dirt build-up is the key. And accountable, honest communication is the strategy to maintain clarity. When the window has mud on it, it is hard to see what is happening on the other side. Being *crystal clear* means there is nothing left on our window and nothing blocking our relationship.

When we are clear and honest with each other we are able to be accountable. I am accountable for my experience. What I choose to think, feel and do is my responsibility even if someone else provided the experience that triggered it. When we are accountable, we are accepting where we are at and can feel worthy right now. If we are not accountable, we are successfully avoiding the feelings wrong and alone for a moment. But we will never feel worthy and accepted because we are not present to where we are at.

When we can forgive ourselves for what we choose to experience we can fully forgive others in our relationships. We can be present to what you and they experienced. When we are present, what you think, feel and do makes perfect sense. There is no mystery behind it. If you could map out all of your experiences and what you chose to think, feel and do, the next step would make perfect sense. What the other person did would make perfect sense.

Forgiveness is seeing ourselves or others as worthy and accepted where they are. *Worthy* does not mean they do good things, but they are valuable even if they are not adding value. *Accepted* is not accepting what they do to you, but accepting that they are where they are and a lifetime of previous experiences explains their behavior. If you have ever forgiven someone, you have gone through this process. You have seen them as someone who is just like you, seeking to be worthy and accepted. They believe their experiences are telling them they are not worthy and accepted so they are trying to prove that they are not wrong and alone.

When you can forgive yourself and be present to what others are experiencing, you will sense what others are thinking and feeling by looking at what they do. You may not know the exact experiences they have had in their life but you'll know what they have been experiencing.

If you understand their core motives, how they create and what they have experienced, you will no longer have to defend yourself. You will not be hurt when they seek to hurt you. You wisely won't allow others to attack you, but you will be more concerned about them than about being offended.

Conscious Creation

A simple example of physical creation is to plant a garden. You choose the plot. You prepare the soil. You choose the seeds. You plant and nurture them. You work and toil and after repeating that for the growing season, you harvest the fruits of your labor. But what about the early frost that threatens to kill everything off? What about the bugs that infest the young leaves? What about the deer that tries to eat everything before it can grow? Well, what about them? You get to choose. Do you want a garden? Do you want the fruit and vegetables? Then, choose it. And create what you want: a productive garden, despite the frost and bugs and deer. Your efforts were focused. You were vigilant and committed to protecting your investment.

Creation, like a garden, is not a magic wand situation. Think of who and what you value most in your life—these relationships and experiences demand the creative capacity to choose.

Mental creation follows the same principles. You choose what you want to experience. You choose your thoughts. You prepare yourself to listen to your conscience so you can change your thoughts to serve you better or keep them to serve you best. You choose your actions. You nourish yourself with your worthiness and acceptance. You work with your imagination and intelligence to understand what is happening and see what is possible. Then you have the power to create what you want. You get to harvest the intangibles despite people around you trying to stop you or hurt you or block you from your dreams. Perhaps you create what you want because of the seeming obstacles that were in your way. You create with focused, vigilant and committed effort to choose. Conscious creation is a powerful play.

PLAY 13: CONSCIOUS CREATION

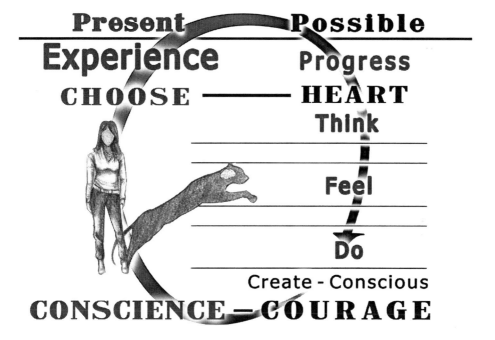

Conscious creation is the ability to choose what we think, feel and do. This play boosts your courage because you have to courageously choose. You're not floating along, experiencing your life through inertia or the path of least resistance. You are courageously and consciously creating. Consciousness is creation's companion because being present to your previous, current and possible experiences gives you power to not be limited by them. Creation means looking out into what's possible and then choosing exactly what you want. You are not contained or restrained by yourself or others. You get to create what you want.

This play means identifying the many available options and choosing the one you want in your life with regard to your thoughts, feelings and actions. Practice the creation play by choosing an experience and listing as many possible thoughts you could have about it as possible. It's best to start with something easy that happens to you often. Write what is possible and follow each thought up with possible feelings and actions that could accompany it. You can also write what possible actions you want in your life and work backwards. Write what feelings and thoughts accompany those actions so that you can get what you want.

Join the **www.5Habits.me** community to see what others are experiencing for Play 13.

CHAPTER 14

Choose Your Culture
Now You Can Teach and Mentor Others

"Everyone has untapped creativity. The mistake many managers make is trying to instill or install creativity into people, rather than removing the interference (fears, uncertainty and negative voices) that blocks it."

~Alan Fine

After we experience the *5 habits* for ourselves, we can then teach, coach or mentor others to create shared values, common core goals and team or organizational culture. This is the role of leaders—to choose the culture that best suits the organization.

A *culture* is what a group of people think, feel and do. It is why, what and how all people think, feel and do. Sadly, fear supplants trust as the primary motivation in most cultures; in fact, most bosses use the fear of being fired to keep order. Cultures built on fear may survive—even thrive for a time, but they become increasingly ineffective. Scared people spend more time plotting their survival than being productive. Individuals, teams and organizations are more successful when they are encouraged to take risks, explore new ideas and channel their energies in ways that work for them. This leadership style is built on trust and inspiration, not fear, and has zero tolerance for bullies, vicious gossip, undermining behaviors, hijacking tactics, political jockeying for position or favoritism. We need to manage and lead organizations based on the emotions that create energy and direct cooperation.

The delivery system for these habits are threefold: 1) teach yourself, 2) teach another person and 3) teach a group of 3 or more people.

To move to steps 2 and 3, we must first be experienced with step 1 ourselves. Only then are we able to give others (teams, groups and organizations) the tools to change for themselves.

Level 3: Groups

The head-to-heart framework is a way to deliver what we think in our head to what we feel in our heart. We know we should do a lot of things, but we don't have the matching feeling behind it. This is because of our personal experiences. If our personal experience is one that puts us in our heart, we will keep doing it. If our experience puts us in our head, we will stop doing it.

Use the head-to-heart framework to choose your experience and assist others to have the freedom to choose their experience. This can happen in any group you are part of. Most groups have a way of thinking and feeling in common that causes a group of people to come together. This is the way they do things together. The head-to-heart framework can be used to assess where the group presently is, where they have previously been and where they could possibly go.

Using the head-to-heart framework in groups empowers members to go to the next level and supports them in having the experience they want to have. Of course, *choosing your culture* is challenging because you are not the only one choosing. I find that the best way to support others in choosing the culture you desire is to have them experience it. That is, they first experience the difference between present culture and possible and then become co-creative change agents to establish a new normal.

Choose your Culture

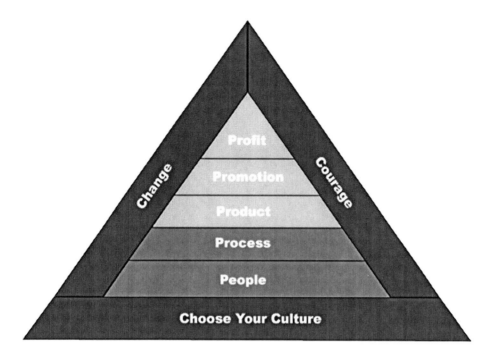

The outside edges of *choose your culture* is the head-to-heart framework. On the left you see what needs to be changed and on the right where you can have courage. Use this framework with your team just like you use it for yourself. As you become *present* to what your culture is choosing, you can see what needs to change and then exercise the courage to consciously create that change.

5 P's of the Culture Pyramid

There are **5 P's of the culture pyramid:** *people, process, product, promotion* and *profit.*

People are the base of any culture. All change comes from people. What they think and feel will determine what they do. If the base is solid, the rest will work out. Unfortunately, we rarely work on the base because it is unseen, unmeasurable and hard to change. This is the work of the head-to-heart framework that creates change.

Process is the next level, which is less visible. Processes only work when people are on board with the culture. We often believe we just need the right process and everything will run on auto-pilot. The problem is that our processes are constantly updating, and that change comes from people—people first, dynamic processes next. The processes must be *repeatable* and *scalable*. It must be so repeatable that someone new can step in and do exactly what was done the day before. The process must be intricately outlined so that it is not dependent on the person. The process must also be *scalable* meaning that if your business expanded, the next new office could also use your processes. They are not dependent on a specific person's personality.

Products are the visible area of culture. This is what everyone sees. How good your products can be is largely based on the people and processes behind them. But it is easy to get caught up in what can be measured—the visible side is the product.

Promotion is part of growth and a lot of time is spent here because it is closely linked to profit. When people, processes and products are aligned, the promotion is sustainable. You need to keep getting better, but it is not the only focus of moving forward.

Profit is the fruition of promoting your product. This is why we are so focused on these top three layers. It is the fast way to the end result. Unfortunately, that is only the case for a short time. Remember the low hanging fruit to harvest? After it is gone you have to up the effort.

This 5-P framework of the culture pyramid helps you see where you are, what needs to change, what you can create on each level and what you're experiencing that holds you back.

There will be many things to change and to create on each of the 5 P's, so it is a matter of doing it over and over again. It will be just like it is with doing the process for yourself. You will enjoy the change and be a conscious creator and show others how to do the same.

Mentoring Others

What makes some people great mentors is their ability to understand what they have experienced and how they have moved through it so they can do the same for others. We can become such mentors if we pay the price to personally experience this head-to-heart process.

Mentoring is how to deliver personal experiences that give ourselves and others the courage to change. I see this as a three-step process:

Step 1: Listen to your conscience by mentoring yourself.

Step 2: Show someone else how to change using the head-to-heart process.

Step 3: Have the same change experience with the team or group.

Mentoring is a valuable but largely forgotten leadership competency. We have coaches who hold us accountable for what we say we will do. We have consultants who tell us what to do. We have speakers who inform and inspire us and trainers who go in depth with content.

Coaching, consulting, speaking and training are all great ways to help others learn knowledge and skills, and yet these activities fall short when it comes to helping others personally experience change for themselves.

Mentoring is taking someone through the experience step by step. Remember the dogs that learned to lay down in the experiment? After being unable to stop the electric shock, they laid down and accepted their fate. Even when a new opportunity came to easily escape the shock, they had to be walked through how to jump over the small barrier. And it is not just based on your experience but based on their experience, recognizing that they have their own unique experiences and unique life journey.

Using a road map from an expert is very helpful. We have become great map makers of what the view is from above. However, personally walking beside people as they chart their own course is where real change happens.

Helping them to navigate by using the compass of their conscience helps sustain the change.

We are transitioning from an information age to an experience age. It is not just external experience but we crave to experience change internally. You already have the perfect mentor with you—your conscience. It knows where you are and where you need to be. My goal is for you to experience using your conscience so that you can mentor yourself and go show others how to do the same. As more people gain the ability to mentor themselves and mentor others we can then learn from one another's experiences without having to experience the pain on our own.

Mobile Mentoring: I have created an overall master play that provides Mobile Mentoring. It is a service that prompts you to report what you are experiencing. It is the easiest way to use the *5 Habits to Lead from Your Heart* and head-to-heart framework to become present in minutes. We are often so busy that we do not take the time to become present and choose our experience. This does it for you automatically and records your progress so you can see how far you have come. It also creates a community of people to learn from.

Again, I invite you to go to **www.5Habits.me** and to use the Mobile Mentoring master play freely as you experience this book.

PLAY 14: CHOOSE YOUR CULTURE

Since *culture* is what a group of people think, feel and do, you gain influence as a leader by changing what all constituents or stakeholders in the organization are thinking, feeling and doing. It is imperative to be accurately aware of what others around you are thinking, feeling and doing. Being present to your current culture means you can realistically influence change. This play is executed by gathering information from those around you, simultaneously helping others articulate what they are experiencing, becoming present to where they are.

Progress in a culture means feeling satisfied. Halting progress brings feelings of dissatisfaction and frustration. Pinpointing the thoughts that accompany easily identifiable feelings helps to identify the starting point for change in a culture. For this play, find out answers from other members of your culture: *have you ever been frustrated or dissatisfied by the people in our culture? The Processes? The Products? The Profits? What were you thinking at those times? What possibilities do you suggest to improve?*

Outcomes are easily measured. Measuring other people's thoughts and feelings takes more work, more connection and time. This valuable information helps you assess the culture accurately.

First, complete the following exercise for yourself regarding your view of your culture. Then, poll members of your team to establish where you are at as a culture. Note the differences and find out the reasoning behind the different perspectives.

On a scale of 1 to 7, what is our performance in the following areas? 1 being the lowest performance possible and 7 being the highest performance possible.

Why is it that number? What needs to change? What could we create?

Profit	1	2	3	4	5	6	7
Promotion	1	2	3	4	5	6	7
Product	1	2	3	4	5	6	7
Process	1	2	3	4	5	6	7
People	1	2	3	4	5	6	7

You can use this strategy to gather general perspectives on each of the 5 P's or you can drill down to get specific about each P. For example, how is our culture performing in our online promotion for this specific product?

Macro and micro perspectives from many team members will give important insights into the efficacy and efficiency of your current culture.

Join the ***www.5Habits.me*** community to see what others are experiencing for Play 14.

CHAPTER 15

Start Your Rebellion
Exercise Courage to Create a New Normal

"First they ignore you, then they ridicule you, then they fight you and then you win."

~Mahatma Gandhi

Y ou can make these *5 habits* your own by starting your own rebellion in your own culture. Since a culture is how a group of people think, feel and what they do, any time your culture is in opposition to what is normal, you are in a state of rebellion. *Healthy rebellion* means moving forward, acknowledging all the while that there is a possibility to produce in a better way. You are breaking free from the familiarity of control and from the comfort of fitting in. You are no longer being controlled by your parents, peers, leaders, teachers, bosses or bullies.

By suggesting that you *start your own rebellion*, I am not suggesting you rebel against that which is good and is healthy for you: your family, team, organization or society. Hopefully you left that sort of rebellious behavior behind when you grew out of teenage rebellion.

Rebelling is an important way to get the most out of life. Teenagers are on the right track, but sometimes they just throw everything out the window. Think of the nose ring, leather clad, mohawk teenager that you are afraid to send your daughter out the door with. Why is she so excited? Because she's pushing back against the norm. Why is he so proud of his look? Because he's exploring how to be different.

Sometimes in that space between childhood and adulthood when you are able to choose for yourself, but you don't know how yet, you are disrespectful and not trying your best. Teenagers get a bad rap for exercising their freedom to choose, but I think in many instances, adults swing too far the other way. *Don't be different. Don't stand out. Don't make waves. Conform. Fit in. Do it the way it has always been done.* Respectful rebellion is actually an important skill to be able to progress. I suggest you rebel against norms that do not allow you to choose. Most of the time rebellion is first an internal battle of us choosing to set ourselves free which can lead to us doing the same for others.

Think of Courageous Rebels

Think of the courageous rebels who have gone before us, and think of the possibilities they created because they weren't willing to be constrained by mankind's previous experiences.

Consider the story of Ignaz Semmelweis, a Hungarian physician who specialized in washing hands while caring for postpartum mothers. It was common for postpartum infections to spread throughout obstetrical clinics, claiming the lives of many women. Semmelweis reduced the mortality rate from over 10 percent to less than 1 percent in his clinics! He was saving 9 more lives out of every 100. It seems like a no-brainer for other doctors of the era to start doing whatever he was doing except he was rejected for going against the norm. Doctors at that time found it insulting to wash their hands. How could they be killing patients? They were there to treat and save them. They had no idea that they could spread disease from patient to patient.

Semmelweis worked hard to convince his cohort to change their behavior but they would not listen to the evidence. Washing hands saves lives. His career was literally ruined because he refused to back down about the efficacy of hand washing. You should research his life. Everyone thought he was crazy for thinking differently. He ended up dying in a mental hospital after being tricked to be admitted. Talk about feeling wrong and alone! It's a miracle Semmelweis persisted in what he did. And Louis Pasteur (think pasteurization) followed up on his work with the germ theory of disease. Too bad it was 20 years after Semmelweis died.

Power of Rebellions

Rebellions are powerful because they break through the old way of doing things so that new ways of thinking can emerge. New ways of thinking often produce exponential new results.

You must start your rebellion with yourself—to question what you think, to look at what you are feeling and what it is telling you to do. Unless you do this, you might understand what I have shared, but you will not experience it.

I don't believe I can inspire you to choose to take the path for yourself. I believe it has to come from within you—something you choose, despite your previous thoughts and feelings.

When we understand what our feelings are telling us, we don't have to go against them. When we are controlled by them or seek them for comfort, then we need to let go of those thoughts and we are able to consciously create a new possibility.

I feel so inadequate when it comes to putting words on paper compared to what I have experienced myself. My fear is that you will conceal your pain so you do not have to change. I understand why you would do this and at the same time, you know what to do.

Before reading this, you may have been honestly able to say *I don't know how*. You are beyond that now. You know how. You can honestly say *I have not experienced it*. Until you do experience it, I realize you will not change and that is all part of this process. The key is acknowledging that you want to change, that you are willing to put in the work.

I believe if we were to let ourselves feel, we would be willing to pay the price to change. The problem is that we know how to not feel and that keeps us from changing. You do not need to wait until a tragedy hits. Commit to have the courage to change now.

Let my words echo in your mind the next time you repeat a process that causes you pain, telling you to change. Let these words bring you not to shame but to change. Let them bring to your mind the truth of who you are and what you are capable of being and doing.

Let your pain tell you that you were born for more and prepared by life experiences to show others the way to be set free. Once you can choose your experience, you can mentor others to do the same. Don't be surprised if they resist at first or if they don't respond or even if they fight against it. They are where they are, and to move forward they need to take the next step.

Plan Your Personal Rebellion

To help you choose your personal experiences and track your progress, I have created the *Personal Experience Planner* (PEP).

Living the *5 Habits to Lead from Your Heart* boils doing to doing one thing: be present and use the head-to-heart framework to consciously create change. This planner gives you the ability to plan what you will choose to do as well as what you will choose to think and feel.

Many planners focus on *do*. The PEP is unique in that it focuses first on *think* and *feel*. It shifts away from having you place heavy emphasis on completing a to-do list toward having you first list what to think and to feel in order to wisely *choose your experience*.

DATE *June 30*		**CHOOSE 1ST**
EXPERIENCE *Peer Evaluation*	**6** *Stretch, breathe, treadmill*	*Anniversary phone call*
HEAD	**7** *Breakfast/Shower*	
THINK *This guy has no idea what I do*	**8**	
FEEL *misunderstood, judged, wrong*	**9** *Team Powow*	
DO *Give him the silent treatment*	**10**	
HEART	**11**	
THINK *This guy might have some insights into me*	**12**	**CONNECT**
FEEL *Nervous, ready*		
DO *Try to apply his suggestions*	**1** *Meet Jim at Steak place*	*Roger* / *Waiting for*
EXPERIENCE	**2** *Confrence call*	*Maintenance Team* / *Sheila*
HEAD	**3**	*Possible sponsors* / *Troy Sales pitch*
THINK	**4** *Profit/Loss presentation*	
FEEL	**5**	**COMMITMENTS**
DO	**6**	*Finalize P & L numbers*
HEART	**7**	*Pick up bouquet, milk, eggs*
THINK	**8** *Dinner reservation*	*Change oil in Maddie's car*
FEEL	**9**	*Bank deposit*
DO		

The basic head-to-heart framework should be used with whatever experience you are focusing on. The times during the day are for your appointments. The first section is *Choose 1st*. This is what is most important, regardless of how urgent it is. The second section is *Connect*. This is who you need to connect with on the left and who you are waiting to connect with you on the right. The last section is *Commitments*. These are things you are committed to do, no matter what. You might have a few tasks you are working on underneath *Commitments*.

PLAY 15: START YOUR REBELLION

The best way to experience the head-to-heart restoration is through your rebellion. Display the head-to-heart framework in a prominent place for you to reference from: desk, fridge, locker, journal, etc. Give the other copy of the framework to someone else and explain what you understand about the framework and what was most powerful for you from what you've learned. As you have daily experience, you can apply the framework to record and ponder your experience and then use your imagination and intelligence to think of what you might consciously create by changing what you think, feel and do. The truth will set you free.

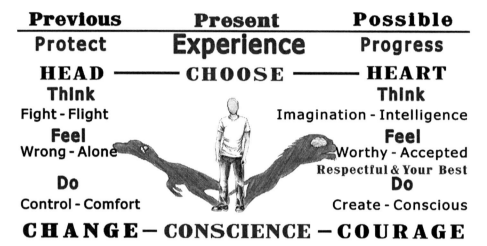

Previous	**Present**	**Possible**
Protect	**Experience**	Progress

HEAD ——— **CHOOSE** ——— **HEART**

Think		**Think**
Fight - Flight		Imagination - Intelligence
Feel		**Feel**
Wrong - Alone		Worthy - Accepted
		Respectful & Your Best
Do		**Do**
Control - Comfort		Create - Conscious

CHANGE— CONSCIENCE —COURAGE

Join the *www.5Habits.me* community to see what others are experiencing for Play 15.

My Promise to You

I promise if you will use the head-to-heart framework over and over, the principles and plays will become part of your way of thinking, feeling and doing. You will feel worthy and accepted because you are choosing your experience—a powerful way to live and lead! If you are dissatisfied with anything in your life, start using the head-to-heart framework in your healthy rebellion. You can make this framework completely yours and fully express your heart then tell me about it at *www.5Habits.me*. Also, I invite you to go to *www.5Habits.me* for additional tools and resources to apply what you have experienced within this book.

CONCLUSION

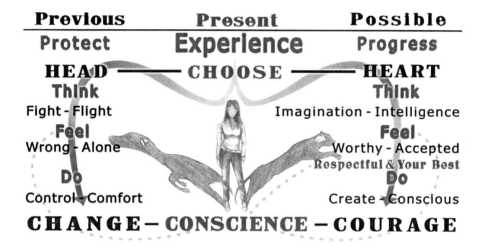

Previous	Present	Possible
Protect	**Experience**	Progress
HEAD ——	CHOOSE ——	**HEART**
Think		**Think**
Fight - Flight		Imagination - Intelligence
Feel		**Feel**
Wrong - Alone		Worthy - Accepted
		Respectful & Your Best
Do		**Do**
Control - Comfort		Create - Conscious

CHANGE — CONSCIENCE — COURAGE

In the *present*, we have an *experience* and there are two primary ways to choose to *think*, *feel* and *do* something about that *experience*.

When we *choose* to *experience* with our *head*, we are using the lower-back brainstem and cerebellum, whose primary purpose is to *protect* us so we become like *raptors* and see others as *raptors*. We think in terms of *fight* or *flight*. With these thoughts we feel *wrong* and *alone*. It does not *feel* good, so in order to not *feel* this way, we seek *control* or *comfort*. This gives us temporary relief from our *feelings* of being *wrong* and *alone*.

When we *choose* to *experience* with our *heart*, we are using our left and right brain with its primary purpose to *progress*. So we become like a *lion* or *lioness*, powerful and able to create what we want and see others in the same way. We *think* using our *imagination* and *intelligence*. With these *thoughts*, we *feel worthy* and *accepted* because we are *being respectful* to ourselves and others and *being our best* which brings us to *being conscious creators.*

Our *conscience* uses our *feelings* to send us messages. When we are in our *heads* our *feelings* are telling us to *change* to *protect* us and when we are in our *heart* the *feelings* are telling us to have *courage* to *progress.*

The reason it is hard to *change,* even though our *feelings* are telling us to, is because we have had *previous experiences* in our heads where we were not *being respectful* or *being our best.* We have not understood what those *feelings* were telling us, so we repeat the *experience.* We thought our *feelings* were telling us that something is *wrong* with us and that we are *alone.* In reality, our painful feelings are telling us that something is *wrong* with our *thought* process and we should leave it *alone.* Our painful experiences happen over and over until we choose to experience a new *possibility* by listening to our *conscience* to *change.* We *change* by having the *courage* to be in our *heart.*

These are a few paragraphs summarizing what you are *experiencing* over and over every day. When you understand it and make it yours, you can *choose* to *experience* it for yourself. You can then experience something different in any area of your life.

Core Concepts and My Belief

My greatest desire is to give you the tools you need to *consciously create change* in any area of your life—to teach you the pattern of how to do this so whether or not you remember the exact flow of the framework or even an example you loved, you will know the pattern of becoming present to your conscience to use the head-to-heart framework.

I want to go over some concepts so that you can apply them.

Each of us is worthy and accepted regardless of our experiences. We are just as worthy and accepted now as we were as a baby. The only difference is the experiences we have had and whether we choose to follow our conscience. When we do follow our conscience, every experience we have moves us towards feeling worthy and accepted. Even painful experiences communicate our worth and acceptance, because they are telling us we are worth it to change.

With experiences that have happened previously we can become present to what we were thinking, feeling and doing using our head and what we could possibly think, feel and do leading from our heart. This will restore this experience to align with our conscience. When we do this with our previous experiences over and over, we are then restored to who we have been all along. To change what we do, we must first change what we think and feel. Focus on think and feel. Be vigilant about examining your thoughts and your feelings. They serve a vital purpose. We do this by becoming present to what we are experiencing in our head previously and what we could experience in our heart, the possible. Doing this creates a new way we choose to have that experience.

We feel worthy when we show ourselves and others respect. We feel accepted when we are being our best and letting others be their best. What we desire more than anything is to feel worthy and accepted and we are the only ones who can give that feeling to ourselves. Being worthy and accepted is our birthright and we can experience this at any moment by choosing it.

We deliver an experience to others by getting them present to what they are experiencing in what they think, feel and do, what they have been experiencing previously and what they will experience as a possibility in the future. This is done by using *think, feel and do* (1,2,3).

Think: Tell them the information they need.

Feel: Give them examples so they can visualize themselves using the information.

Do: Then have them experience it for themselves.

1. Mentor themselves by exploring and expressing their experience.

2. Mentor one other person what you discovered.

3. Implement it in a group of 3 or more. This could be in a work, family or social setting. This is where you choose a new experience.

Another way to say that is 1) teach yourself, 2) teach another person and 3) teach a group of 3 or more people.

They will have learned from you and received examples (think and feel), taught themselves and one other person, been taught one-on-one by another person and implemented it within a group. All of this leads them to use this experience—experience is the master teacher. In the future when they have feelings they might otherwise overlook, they will examine the thought that preceded the feeling to know if they want to courageously continue or change.

I believe that all principles and natural laws are governed by a higher power. The more we understand, the more it makes sense because it is all by design. In my opinion, this higher power has many names: nature, the universe, Khuda, God, Allah, science, Vishnu, Heavenly Father. Regardless of your belief of what this higher power is called or what they are like, I think it is important to explain my belief on how and why our conscience is directly aligned with principles and natural laws.

At the center of all principles and natural laws is conscience. It is at the center because for each of us personally, it is how we experience these natural laws and principles. Our conscience is our personal barometer letting us know when we are aligned with principles and natural laws. When we are not aligned, it sends a message through our feelings that we need to change. When we are aligned, it sends a message through our feelings that we need to be courageous. Either way, our conscience is trying to keep us aligned with principles and natural laws so that we can grow.

This is why our conscience is a conduit to our higher power. It is how our higher power communicates to us to be aligned with the principles and natural laws they have designed. You may not believe that this higher power is God, like I do. Regardless of how you experience this higher power or if you believe there is one or not, I hope you can see that this structure is in place to align us to principles and natural laws.

If the principles of the head-to-heart framework are aligned with natural laws it will work every time. The practices will change for each of us but the principles will not. Test these principles out for yourself so you can personally experience them. If they are aligned with natural laws like I have said, it means you can use them to choose your experience regardless of what you have experienced. The only thing really required of you is your willingness to follow these principles.

If your heart resonates with this message join me in this rebellion.

APPENDIX

LANGUAGE OF THE HEAD-TO-HEART FRAMEWORK

Learning the *5 habits* is the mental and emotional equivalent of learning a new language. With the alphabet, you can create thousands of words. With those words, you can create sentences to express what you are experiencing and understand the experience of others. The head-to-heart framework provides a language that enables you to express clearly what you are experiencing and also clearly understand the experience of others.

Many of the words I use to describe the plays of this game of life are familiar, but the usage or definition may be different. Here are the head-to-heart framework definitions and an accompanying explanation.

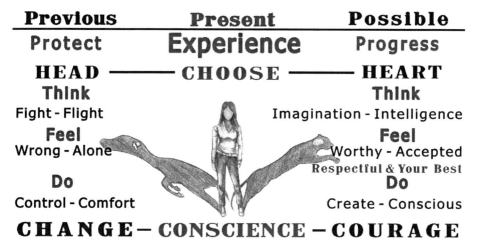

Previous	Present	Possible
Protect	**Experience**	Progress

HEAD ——— CHOOSE ——— **HEART**

Think
Fight - Flight

Think
Imagination - Intelligence

Feel
Wrong - Alone

Feel
Worthy - Accepted
Respectful & Your Best

Do
Control - Comfort

Do
Create - Conscious

CHANGE — CONSCIENCE — COURAGE

Experience: something that happens to us. What we experience is something that we consciously create as we make choices and apply principles.

Principles: timeless truths that work in every instance.

Practices: how we apply principles.

Truth: reality based on principles.

Choice: the ability to freely think, feel and do regardless of what you experience.

Think, Feel, Do (TFD): what we experience is the result of what we choose to think, feel and do about our experience.

Wrong: we feel wrong when we feel disconnected from ourselves.

Alone: we feel alone when we feel disconnected from others.

Worthy: we feel worthy when we feel valuable regardless of previous experience.

Accepted: we feel accepted when we feel that we are enough, regardless of previous experience.

Change: we change when we begin to think, feel and do differently.

Head: we are in our head when we use our brain for a fight/flight response (lower-back brainstem and cerebellum) also termed our **raptor** response.

Fight or Flight: being in our head prompts protective behaviors; fight protects us by force, flight protects us by fleeing or avoidance.

Raptor: to protect ourselves we become like a raptor or feel like others are raptors. This enables us to survive by fight or flight by using our head to protect our heart.

Control or Comfort: Being in our head also drives us to seek either control or comfort. Control is when we are manipulating our experience to gain temporary relief from pain. Comfort is when we are avoiding our experience to gain temporary relief from pain.

Using our head, we take two primary paths: we think with fight, then we feel wrong and seek control, or we think with flight, then we feel alone and seek comfort. Often when we feel one of these emotions the other emotion follows. We can feel both emotions in fight or flight mode.

Heart: we are in our heart when we are using our imagination and intelligence (neocortex, or right/left brain) to consciously create what we experience.

Imagination: our ability to see possibility.

Intelligence: our ability to understand experience.

Courage: the ability to choose to follow your conscience regardless of what you are experiencing.

Lion: when we are being courageous, we are like a lion, choosing to consciously create our own experiences in order to feel worthy and accepted.

Conscience: our internal voice that communicates through our emotions. Our conscience guides us to choose the experience that will help us progress.

Conscious: being conscious is being present to where we have previously been, where we presently are and where we can possibly go. This is how we progress.

Creation: the ability to choose what we think, feel and do.

Head-to-heart: Going from our head to our heart restores us to who we really are. We can then experience life as we did when we were children, feeling worthy and accepted.

Habit: a predictable experience of thinking, feeling and behaving (doing).

Heart habit: a predictable experience of thinking, feeling and doing based on principles from the heart.

EXAMPLES OF HEAD-TO-HEART

Daily **exercise** of the head-to-heart process empowers you to choose your life *experiences*. We all have different experiences in terms of what happens to us; however, we all face a similar challenge: to choose our experience by choosing what to think, feel and do.

My hope is that you then become another great example, among many great *examples*, of what you could possibly think, feel and do in regards to experiences you are having.

Be in Your Heart

Being in your heart is to *connect with others in healthy ways*—to have empathy for what others think and feel and to see that those thoughts and feelings trigger them to take certain actions. Rather than being critical, comparing or competing, you are compassionate. You treat others with an abundant mentality—sensing that there is enough to go around and that comradery is more powerful than competition. Your value is not based on having or being more than others.

When you compare or compete in unhealthy ways, you create an unnecessary battle where someone has to be wrong. Connection combats feeling wrong and alone and cultivates creation where you can use your imagination and intelligence from feelings of self-worth.

Recognize when you choose to be in your heart in these two scenarios.

Scenario 1

As you sit in the weekly sales meeting, listening to Stan report on his accounts, you are thinking about the new car he drove to work this morning.

Think: How could he afford that? I know he can't be making more than I am. There is no way I could make the payment on that car.

Feel: I'm completely jealous. I compare myself and what I'm driving and how I'm spending my money and what I'm getting paid to Stan. I know to beware of comparing. I feel comfortable enough with Stan to reach out to connect with him.

Do: When everyone breaks for coffee and donuts, you make a beeline. You recognize your connection with Stan. "Nice wheels, man."

"I thought I saw you envying my car this morning as I came in."

"You caught me. How did you make that happen? I'm stuck in a car with enough seatbelts to keep me out of the cool category. What are you thinking? Is this your mid-life crisis? The insurance alone on that baby would be enough to scare me!"

"Well, I've always wanted to drive it. I've had my eye on it for one year now. I finally just went for it—sink or swim. I'm motivated to burn the midnight oil if it means I can keep it."

"That's showing guts. Congratulations. I definitely want a ride in your car today."

Scenario 2

You are on the playground watching your four-year-old daughter play in the sand and trying to finish up paying some bills from your phone. You see a two-year-old girl swipe Sarah's shovel. You look around to see if any other parent will engage. Sarah is calm about it. She just picks up another shovel and goes back to digging. Your parental pride meter is through the roof. She must have been listening to all of your attempts to teach her to share.

As you are going back to your screen, you hear the wrath of the girl's mother. "Abby! What have I told you about taking other children's toys? No!" Abby is stoic. "Come with me right now. Give that back!" Abby is holding her ground. "You are in serious trouble. Tell her sorry, Abby. Tell her!" Abby has a death grip on the shovel and is determined to keep it. "We are never coming back to this park if you don't apologize right now."

Think: This mom is probably fighting the toy-stealing phase fight. Poor woman! I remember when Sarah would bite any child that tried to recover their own toy. That phase was so hard, and I'm glad it is over. I wonder if she thinks Abby took the shovel out of Sarah's hand. I'm not worried about shovel sharing. I hope she's not thinking I care.

Feel: I feel bad for this mom. Now she's turned this into a standoff, and it doesn't look good for parent or child. I feel relief that my child has grown older. I feel connected to the mom because I know how hard this is.

Do: You stand up from the bench and join the three of them. You recognize your connection with this mom. "It looks like it was an honest mistake. Sarah brought quite a few shovels today. Sarah, what do you think about sharing?"

"I'm okay. The purple shovel is my favorite that I want to use."

"Abby, Sarah is willing to share that orange shovel while we are here at the park. We're staying for 15 more minutes. Would you like to use it until it's time for us to go?"

Abby's mom looks relieved. Abby doesn't talk but nods her head. "Alright, then that's settled. When it's time for us to leave, I will have you put the shovel in our toy bag. Thanks, Abby. I'd say that's amazing for a big girl like you. How old is she?"

Abby's mom has visibly relaxed. "She's two. She likes to take things away from other kids without asking."

"She's looks like she's learning. This age was so hard for us, too! I thought I would never be able to go out in public. It was so bad."

"Right? I'm hoping it gets better."

"It does. Then we'll both have something else to figure out!"

> **Have you ever had someone let you know it's ok to be where you are at?**
>
> *Christine: I sit through 75 minutes of church worship service with young children on one pew. I will never forget a grandmother from my congregation telling me that our loud, noisy and irreverent family was doing just fine.*
>
> **How could you do that for someone else?**
>
> *Christine: I like to wave to moms in the grocery store who have children throwing tantrums. I give them the thumbs up.*

Previous	Present	Possible

Protect   **Experience**   Progress

HEAD ——— **CHOOSE** ——— **HEART**

Think   Think

Feel   Feel
                                                    Empathy

Do   Do

C H A N G E — CONSCIENCE — C O U R A G E

Recognize opportunities to connect. Be in your heart. Take the time to identify feelings of comparison and competition that inhibit connection—and then, choose to think of what the other person might be experiencing. As you practice thinking about others, your personal awareness of others increases, which increases your ability to be in your heart.

BE PRESENT

Being Present is *recognizing what you are experiencing and choosing*—being aware of what you think and feel and what those thoughts and feelings typically trigger you to do. For example, when you are in your head, you often have *enmity,* a feeling of hatred or hostility, for others; when you are in your heart, you tend to have *empathy,* the ability to understand and share the feelings of others. You may have many of the same thoughts, feelings and actions, but when you lead from your heart, you get much better results.

Recognize when you are present in your head and in your heart in the following two scenarios—or in other scenarios you might imagine:

Scenario 1

The driver in front of you is sitting at the light after it's turned green. Cars in the lanes around you are moving forward, but you are stopped behind this car. It looks like the driver is texting. What are you experiencing? What are you thinking, feeling and doing?

Thinking with your head: I think I am late. I don't have time for this guy. I think he is inconsiderate. I think he should learn some manners and practice safe driving.

Thinking with your heart: I think I can make it around him safely. I think about yesterday when I got a few honks for sitting at that red light when I should have turned right. I was totally distracted.

Feeling with your head: I feel annoyed. I feel angry. I feel impatient.

Feeling with your heart: I feel empathy for the distracted driver. I feel connection for our common experience. I feel patient and able to get what I want.

Doing with your head: I honk my horn and look for a window in the passing cars to get around this guy and on with my day. I find the window, punch on the gas and give the guy a mean look. He is still just sitting there oblivious to the hold-up he created.

Doing with your heart: I look for an opening in the passing cars, signal and merge, smile as I go by and get on with my day. He is oblivious to the hold-up he created.

Scenario 2

You are waiting for your teenager to come home. It is a school night, and the family rule is to be home by 9 p.m. You have tried calling, but your call goes straight to voicemail. You check her grades online and see that they are worse than what she reported (and she used grades to gain the privilege of going out on a school night in the first place). Finally, at 9:45 you see her friend drop her off in front of the house and drive away.

What are you experiencing? What are you thinking, feeling and doing?

Thinking with your head: I think this is the third time this has happened this month. I think she is being disrespectful and ungrateful for the privileges I provide her. I think she is doing this on purpose. I think she knows how to push my buttons. I think she doesn't even care.

Thinking with your heart: I think there must be something going on for her that I have no idea about. I think she and I can figure this out together.

Feeling with your head: I feel disappointed and frustrated. I feel furious. I feel betrayed because she lied to me. I feel nervous about how to handle her explosion over the consequences I give her.

Feeling with your heart: I still feel disappointed but also a deep sense of love and desire to do what is best for her.

Doing with your head: I start yelling before the front door is closed behind her. I can't even remember everything I said but I screamed *Don't you ever do that again!* And *I'll show you not to lie to me!* I tell her she is grounded for the next month and to turn in her cell phone.

Doing with your heart: I open the door to meet my daughter. I can tell from the look on her face that she feels bad. I don't say a word, but I give her a hug. To my surprise, she starts sobbing and apologizing. She lets me know about the drama going on between her and her boyfriend. This conversation tonight had ended with deciding to break up.

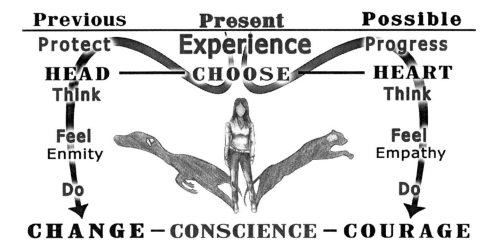

CHANGE – CONSCIENCE – COURAGE

That's how you choose your experience. Simply ask yourself what you were thinking, feeling and doing in any given situation. Take the time to pause and examine what you are experiencing—being present to your thoughts, feelings and actions. Eventually, you can improve your proficiency to choose your experience so that you can stop in the middle of an experience to identify what you are experiencing. While something is happening to you, you can ask yourself what you are thinking and feeling before you commit to doing something. As your skills improve, you can quickly decode the messages your conscience is telling you through your feelings as you are feeling them instead of analyzing your feelings after the fact.

CHOOSE YOUR EXPERIENCE

Your thoughts, feelings and actions come from your choices. Choosing your experience means stopping to examine what you are experiencing and exploring other choices—if you want to experience something different.

For example, suppose that your mother-in-law sends invitations to the extended family to attend Thanksgiving dinner—in January! She is pressuring everyone to be there, and she reminds you that you missed Christmas last year because you took your family to Disneyland.

First, what are you experiencing?

Think: I think these passive-aggressive invitations are over the top. I think this is the reason I don't enjoy being at my wife's family events. I think my wife agrees with me. I think I had a good reason for missing Christmas because we were focused on our family. Our daughter Annie turned 9, and we wanted to go while she still thought it was magical.

Feel: I feel annoyed. I feel angry. I feel judged. I feel like I'm never going to do it right, so why try? I feel trapped. I feel like no matter what I do, I'm wrong.

Do: Before you do anything about it, stop to find out why your conscience sent you that specific feeling. What thought is your conscience telling you to examine? Are your feelings telling you to have courage to change or continue? Remember what your feelings are: annoyed, angry, judged, trapped, wrong.

Why are you annoyed? Because this is annoying! And this is not the first time she has been passive aggressive. Mothers shouldn't guilt-trip their children into action. You don't want to guilt your children into action. You want to be sensitive to what they need. She's wrong.

Why are you angry? Because this is not the first time she has been disrespectful. You don't want to be disrespectful. You don't want someone else to feel this way that you are feeling right now. You are right about this.

Why did you feel judged? Because she wants to do every holiday her way. It isn't right for her to try to control her family. Now you know what it feels like when someone tries to control you so you refuse to deal that way with those that you love. You are not wrong.

Why did you feel trapped? Because she is only giving me one choice for Thanksgiving dinner. It seems like I owed her a holiday, but holidays should be enjoyable and freely chosen. Now you know what it feels like when someone keeps score so you refuse to keep score with those you love. You refuse to make someone feel wrong.

Why did you feel wrong? Because you made a choice and she didn't approve. Now she wants you to change and do it her way. Are you wrong? No. Are you willing to try your best and be respectful? Your conscience is trying to tell you that something is wrong. What is wrong here? What should you have the courage to change and/or the courage to continue? If we don't examine the feelings that convey the message from our conscience, we could misinterpret our feelings. And when we choose actions based on wrong information, someone usually gets hurt.

Do: Based on what you are experiencing, identify possible choices for what you could do: I could ignore the invitation and go to Disneyland again for Thanksgiving this year. I could be angry about this, not speak to my mother-in-law and avoid all possible family interaction. I could book tickets to my family for Thanksgiving and tell her we didn't know. I could just go along with everything until the day before Thanksgiving, I can feign a work emergency.

After brainstorming what your conscience was trying to tell you through your feelings, you can see other possibilities. What could I possibly think, feel and do?

Possibly think: I could think that my mother-in-law's invitation is her way of being prepared. I could think that she loves us and wants us to all be together once a year. I could think of how she sent Disneyland spending money for each of the kids when we went last Christmas. I could think that she cares about each of us being together since my father-in-law had that heart scare last year. I could think that we can figure this out if I have the courage to be honest.

Possibly feel: I could feel love and appreciation for the woman who raised my wife. I could feel grateful for the chance my children have to be loved by so many grandparents. I could feel wanted and included. I could feel excited for her cooking. I could feel respected because she was considerate to plan so far in advance. I could feel excited to clarify any miscommunications.

Possibly do: I could talk to my mother-in-law about why we missed Christmas. She obviously took it personally. I could talk to my wife about it to see what her insights are. I could talk to her other siblings and see where they weigh in on Thanksgiving. I could tell my mother-in-law we would like to host everyone for Thanksgiving to switch things up.

As you can see, the possible choices are endless. Now, pick an experience you have had and work through the choices that are available. What will you choose to think, feel and do?

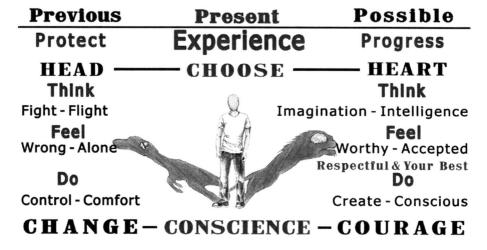

Previous	**Present**	**Possible**
Protect	**Experience**	Progress

HEAD —— **CHOOSE** —— **HEART**

Think		**Think**
Fight - Flight		Imagination - Intelligence
Feel		**Feel**
Wrong - Alone		Worthy - Accepted
		Respectful & Your Best
Do		**Do**
Control - Comfort		Create - Conscious

CHANGE — CONSCIENCE — COURAGE

VISION OF HEAD-TO-HEART

The head-to-heart framework was organized by myself and my wife, Christine. The principles and processes were always there. We simply compiled them into a framework and explained what we observed happening. Because of this, the framework does not belong to us alone. It belongs to all of us. Because there is group ownership over it, it also belongs to you.

What that means is: use it like it is yours. Don't get caught up in the fact that you did not organize it. Focus on the fact that you have already been doing it for years. There are three ways you make it your own: 1. Me 2. Mentor 3. Messenger

1. Me (Mentor yourself) Apply it for yourself by incorporating it into your language and your process. Record the experiences you have of going head-to-heart.

2. Mentor (Mentor other people one on one) Share your experience with others and mentor them to use it in their language and their process. Have them record their experiences of going head-to-heart.

3. Messenger (People you have mentored then find others to mentor, who find others to mentor, going on and on) You are then able to use the head-to-heart framework as a tool to deliver your unique message.

If enough people make the head-to-heart framework and process their own, I truly believe it will be something that everyone has access to. My ultimate vision is that the head-to-heart framework and process will provide a universal tool and language to tackle the most challenging problems we face. I would like to outline how we do this together by sharing my purpose, my missions and the result they will bring.

My purpose: To provide every person with the mentors and messengers they will need to choose their experience.

To do this we must create a community that will mentor each other one on one as a direct mentor or to a group as a messenger. My hope is that people passionate about this community will help create it.

My mission: To record our human experience using the head-to-heart framework and process.

Within this community we record our experiences and connect with people having similar experiences. People have experiences in common, but also as it talks about in Chapter 6, Habit 2: Be You, they share the same core motives as well as how they create. As this happens we will no longer feel wrong or that we are alone because we know others have gone from their head to their heart in having the same experience we are having. We can learn from their experiences.

The result: Anyone who is willing, can have the ability to mentor themselves and to be mentored by their conscience.

In the words of Stephen R. Covey the result will be "To educate and obey our conscience." **My purpose** is for everyone to have the mentors they need. **My mission** is that we learn from the experiences of others. As this community uses the head-to-heart framework and process, it will point them to be mentored by their conscience. Ultimately it is only by being mentored by our conscience that we will have the courage to change. When we have this courage to change, if we will be respectful and our best, we will consciously create. This allows us to feel worthy and accepted, which in the end, is all we really want.

This framework is for you to utilize. One way to share your experience and spread this message is to become a head-to-heart mentor. There is no cost to do this and it will support you in being a powerful messenger. All you do is:

1. Me (mentor yourself) Record 21 experiences you have of going head-to-heart.

2. Mentor (Mentor other people one on one) Mentor people to record their 21 experiences of going head-to-heart.

Doing step 1 and step 2 for three people and reporting it makes you a certified Head-to-Heart mentor. Get the tools to mentor yourself, report your 21 experiences and have the 3 people you mentor report their 21 experiences at *www.5Habits.me*

3. Messenger (Spread the head-to-heart process with groups of people) Use the framework with your friends, family and business. Using the head-to-heart framework combined with your unique message as a mentor, teacher, trainer, or speaker enables you to lead from your heart.

ABOUT THE AUTHOR

Johnny Covey is a bright and intelligent leader from a rich heritage of thinkers. Creating is his favorite past time. He specializes in finding the third alternative. His resume includes using his unique problem-solving skills to create in a variety of industries: real estate, insurance, sales training, finance, entertainment, education and food services. Johnny has mentored thousands of individuals, helping them to see what they couldn't see before and providing a framework for change. Johnny is married to his best friend, Christine Davis Covey, and together they are changing and progressing. Together they raise their seven children: two teenage foster daughters and five biological children ages eight and under. Their front yard in Utah is messy with toys and you can hear them blasting Disney songs as they clean up the dinner dishes. The Coveys enjoy road trips and pizza night.

CPSIA information can be obtained at www.ICGtesting.com
Printed in the USA
BVOW05s1954200516

448937BV00001B/1/P